THE CONTEMPORARY CONSUMER SERIES

Understanding the Marketplace

HILLIS K. IDLEMAN, M.A.

Associate in Secondary Curriculum,
Consumer Education Specialist
The State Education Department
Albany, New York

MAX O. McKITRICK, Ed.D.

Professor of Business Education
College of Business
Western Michigan University
Kalamazoo, Michigan

GREGG AND COMMUNITY COLLEGE DIVISION/McGRAW-HILL BOOK COMPANY

New York	*Kuala Lumpur*	*Paris*
St. Louis	*London*	*São Paulo*
Dallas	*Mexico*	*Singapore*
San Francisco	*Montreal*	*Sydney*
Düsseldorf	*New Delhi*	*Tokyo*
Johannesburg	*Panama*	*Toronto*

Library of Congress Cataloging in Publication Data

Idleman, Hillis K   date.
    Understanding the marketplace.

    (The Contemporary consumer)
    SUMMARY: Describes the contemporary marketplace,
the persuasive role of advertising, and current issues facing
the consumer.
    1. Supply and demand. 2. Consumption (Economics)
3.   Advertising.   [1.   Advertising–Psychological aspects.
2. Consumers] I. McKitrick, Max O., date. joint author.
II. Title. [B201.I34] 381 73-22313
ISBN 0-07-031687-2

UNDERSTANDING THE MARKETPLACE

1 2 3 4 5 6 7 8 9 BABA 7 4 3 2 1 0 9 8 7 6 5

*This book was set in Press Roman by Creative Book
Services, a division of McGregor and Werner, Incorporated.   The senior editor was Joseph G. Bonnice,
the designer was Creative Book Services, the production supervisor was Richard Jacobson, the cover designer was Edward Butler, and the illustrator was
Severino Marcelo.*

THE CONTEMPORARY CONSUMER SERIES

PREFACE

Although today's consumers are the best educated in our country's history, they are often unable to cope with sophisticated business personnel and practices—or with their own uncertain values. For these reasons, citizens are demanding that schools offer basic instruction in consumer skills, rights, and responsibilities. Some states have already enacted legislation mandating that instruction in consumer principles and problems be incorporated into the curriculum of all secondary schools; in other states, bills requiring the teaching of consumer education have been proposed by governors and state legislators.

In the past, secondary schools have often offered courses in consumer education on an elective basis. Today, the cry is heard that *all* students should receive the education needed to be effective consumers both as adolescents and as adults.

Consumer education may be presented in various ways in addition to being offered as a full-year or a one-semester course. For instance, it may be integrated into other subjects; it may be taught as separate units in other traditional courses; or it may be offered as a series of mini-courses devoted to specific topics. The series of eight modules that comprise *The Contemporary Consumer* is designed to offer the flexibility needed to present consumer education in any of these ways. Moreover, consumer education often utilizes an interdisciplinary strategy that builds on the strengths of each related discipline—home economics, business education, distributive education, and social studies. The modular format of *The Contemporary Consumer* makes this approach easy to implement.

OBJECTIVES OF UNDERSTANDING THE MARKETPLACE

The module, *Understanding the Marketplace,* provides an orientation to the vast market system in which consumers must fulfill their needs for goods and services. Emphasis is placed on helping consumers to clarify their values and to develop the skills needed for making wise decisions. The students are introduced to the different forces that influence buying practices, especially advertising.

The students are taught to develop both short- and long-range plans for their personal buying. In this connection, they are given guides to the effectiveness and limitations of information provided by public and private consumer testing agencies and bureaus. The students are made aware of the ways in which uncontrolled consumption affects the environment, the resources, and the inhabitants of our country. Finally, the students learn about the rights of redress they may exercise when purchases prove unsatisfactory and about the obligations they must assume if they are to be responsible consumers.

INSTRUCTIONAL CONTENT

The three chapters of *Understanding the Marketplace* discuss topics that consumer educators generally agree are essential for developing effective buying skills. The chapters, together with the topics covered, are given below:

"Psychology, Values, and Decision Making"—the meaning of consumer education; an explanation of the market economy; a determination of how consumers' values affect their decisions; reasons why consumers buy; a discussion of how psychology and advertising influence consumers' decisions; and an analysis of the techniques used by merchants to move merchandise.

"Effective Consumer Behavior"—developing buying plans; acquiring skill as a comparison shopper; understanding labels, grades, guarantees, and other conditions of sale; and utilizing public and private sources of consumer help and information. "Consumer Issues"—pricing practices; the effect of consumption on the environment; the relationship of poor consumer practices to poverty and crime; and consumer rights and responsibilities.

Student interest in these topics is aroused by the use of thought-provoking questions, realistic examples, and attractive illustrations.

LEARNING AND TEACHING AIDS

If a consumer education program is to be effective, it requires more than just up-to-date instructional material; it also requires activities that will give students an opportunity to review and apply what they have learned. In addition, the teachers of the program need instructional materials to support the content of each module.

End-of-Chapter Activities

Two types of activities are found at the end of each chapter. "Checking Your Reading" is a series of questions that require brief written answers based on recall of information presented in the chapter. "Consumer Problems and Projects" requires students to apply what they have learned to practical situations. Some of these problems and projects can be completed individually; others require the participation of a group of students or the entire class. The problems and projects vary in difficulty, thereby enabling the teacher to provide for individual differences among the students.

End-of-Module Activities

Additional activities for each chapter are printed on perforated sheets found at the end of the module. "Language of the Consumer" enables the students to develop their knowledge of the vocabulary of the consumer. "Be a Better Consumer" is an objective activity that enhances the students' understanding of the facts and concepts that have been explained in the chapter. "Consumer Decisions and Issues" requires the students to write solutions to short, practical cases and typical consumer problems, many of which are of a controversial nature. All of these end-of-module activities allow for self-testing before students are evaluated by the teacher.

Teacher's Manual and Key

The *Teacher's Manual and Key* contains answers to all end-of-chapter and end-of-module questions. It also offers practical suggestions for handling activities, projects, demonstrations, and discussions and provides a list of major behavioral objectives for each chapter. In addition, it contains suggestions for using the module to teach consumer education on an individualized basis. An end-of-module objective test, which the teacher is given permission to duplicate, is incorporated into this manual.

General Methodology Manual

The *General Methodology Manual* is a separate publication that supports the entire series and provides recommendations for schedules, curriculum development, and implementation. General behavioral objectives, particularly in the affective domain, are included.

Audiovisual Materials

A set of sound filmstrips correlated with The Contemporary Consumer Series is also available. The filmstrips are particularly useful in building student interest and awareness.

ACKNOWLEDGMENTS

The teachers who participated in graduate seminars on the teaching of consumer education at Western Michigan University and the University of Wyoming made many valuable suggestions that have been utilized in preparation of end-of-chapter and end-of-module activities for this booklet. Their assistance is acknowledged with thanks.

Hillis K. Idleman
Max O. McKitrick

CONTENTS

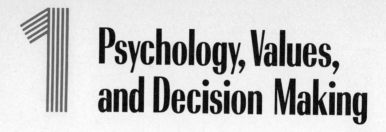

1 Psychology, Values, and Decision Making

Perhaps you are wondering why you should study consumer education. "What's in it for me?" you ask. Your question is a legitimate one, and one that also has a simple answer.

You are a consumer—someone who buys the goods and services you need and want. If you are hungry, for example, you stop off for a hamburger and a milk shake. If your sneakers are now too small for you, you buy a new pair. If you want entertainment, you decide to see a movie or go to a concert. In each case, you exchange money for something you want. Sometimes you may be happy with what you have bought; at other times, however, you may be very disappointed.

The purpose of consumer education, therefore, is to show you how to avoid disappointments with what you buy. You will learn to use the money you have or will earn in a way that will give you satisfaction. Consumer education can help you stretch your dollars to buy more of the things you want. It can show you how to avoid paying more than you should for an item and how to keep from going into debt. You will learn what to do in real-life situations and how to deal with practical financial problems all young people face. For example, what would you do if you found yourself in the following situations?

- You are overcharged in a supermarket.

- You receive unordered merchandise in the mail.

- You do not know which radio or cassette player is the best one to buy.

- You need a car but must borrow money in order to buy it.

- You have money to save or invest.

- You are always buying things you do not really need or want.

- You are thinking about marriage and wondering whether to buy or rent a house.

- You never seem to have enough money to go around.

Money problems like these are shared by millions of Americans. Somehow, there never seems to be enough money available to buy all the things we really want or need. That is why, in thousands of schools, students are now studying consumer education. They are learning, as you will, how to become smart consumers—how to make more intelligent choices when they buy. To do this, of course, young Americans must first learn something about the marketplace and about themselves and their values.

WE LIVE IN A MARKET ECONOMY

The economic system of the United States is sometimes called a "market economy." This is because you, as a consumer, play an important part in determining just what goods and services will be produced.

Let us consider this idea for a moment. Goods and services are bought and sold in the marketplace. That marketplace can be almost anywhere—at your local supermarket, at the box office where you buy a movie ticket, or at the pizza stand where you have lunch. What makes a marketplace is a buyer and a seller, exchanging money for something.

Every time you buy something, you are actually voting for the continued production of that particular product or service. Suppose, for instance, two new breakfast cereals, Marmalade Puffs and Choco-Wheats arrive in your local supermarket at the same time. You buy a box of each, try them, and decide that Marmalade Puffs are terrible, Choco-Wheats delicious. This means that you will continue buying Choco-Wheats, but never spend another cent on Marmalade Puffs. If a number of other consumers make the same decision, the manufacturer of Choco-Wheats will get the message: He will produce more of this particular cereal. The manufacturer of Marmalade Puffs will also get a message. If he is smart, he will concentrate on another product.

It is true that manufacturers decide what to produce, be it a 3-foot-long hot dog, or a three-wheel car. But you do not have to buy what they are trying to sell, and by refusing to buy you can push products you do not like out of the marketplace for good.

A MATTER OF VALUES

Almost everything we do in life depends upon our values. *Values* are the attitudes and opinions we have about the things that are most important to us. They determine the goals that we set for ourselves and the manner and style in which we live.

There are some people, for example, who place great importance on material things. Their goal is to have the most and best of everything. Others consider personal and family relationships most important, and they devote a great deal of time and effort to them. Still other people might place freedom or knowledge or excitement and adventure at the top of the list of things they consider most important.

How are our personal values developed? Well, naturally enough, our earliest values stem from our parents. We see what they consider important, we watch what they buy and how they live, and we tend to imitate them. As we grow older, however, the opinions of our friends and the ideas we receive from television, newspapers, and magazines may assume greater importance. Progressively, we "turn off" some of the values that our parents taught us and "turn on" the values of our friends or people we admire.

For example, a girl might suddenly decide that looking like a famous model is more important than learning to cook. She may diet in order to slim down to ninety pounds, and certainly she will follow the trends in fashion and makeup. Or a boy who once wanted to become a doctor will decide he is more interested in becoming a rock singer. He will cut down on his school work and devote more time to singing and practicing his guitar.

Of course, as we reach adulthood our values may change again, and we will set new goals for ourselves. The security of a good job, the desire to own a home, the need to provide for a family, these. may become far more important than any values or goals we have had previously.

Our personal values have a tremendous influence on us, and nowhere is this more apparent than in the way we spend our money. Our choice of food, recreation, housing, clothing, and education is

Whatever the size of the purchases they make, consumers base their decisions on a complex set of needs and values
Courtesy Burdine's

determined by what we consider important and how we want to live as well as by the amount of money we have available. One man may spend a great deal of money on an expensive house, a fancy car, and meals in the best restaurants. Another may live on a much simpler scale in order to send his children to college. One teen-ager may spend a lot of money on records, another on dating the prettiest girl in the class.

Sometimes we may be willing to give up immediate pleasures or goals in order to achieve more important ones later on. In other words, we do not buy something we want now so that we can get something else later. An example of this would be the teen-ager who decides to save his money in order to go to college. In contrast, another teen-ager, who wants the immediate pleasure of owning a sporty racing car, might end his education at high school graduation and take the first job that will enable him to buy the car.

Questions of conflicting values face us every day. Do we spend the money we now have for a dress, a jacket, a television set, a record? Or do we save it for something we want in the future? The way we answer questions like these will determine how well and how successfully we live our lives.

WHY WE BUY

It is always interesting to get to know ourselves better, to understand why we do what we do. This understanding is particularly important when it touches our "pocketbooks"—our feelings about our money. Everyone takes pleasure in making a good buy or getting a bargain. On the other hand, we are unhappy when we learn that we have been gypped, that what we have bought cost more than it should or fails to give us much satisfaction.

Manufacturers and merchants make a study of buyer behavior and carefully plan their advertising and sales programs to get us to buy their goods. There is nothing wrong with this, of course. If they did not adopt this approach, they would soon go out of business. But just as the merchant studies us and aims his sales efforts toward turning us into customers, so we should try to understand ourselves and to think about our buying habits.

Why do we buy the things we do? As we have already indicated, our personal values and goals play an important part in our buying decisions. In addition, there are a number of other motivating forces or drives that push us into buying. We want to feel good and safe and comfortable. Or we want to feel that we have a certain status in the community, that people approve of us. Perhaps some of us simply want to feel that we can spend money freely, buying anything we see. All these motivating forces put us in a mood to buy and guide us toward the things that will best meet our particular needs.

Physical Well-Being

One of our major needs is for physical well-being. When we are hungry, for example, we seek food. When we are thirsty, we want something to drink. When we feel sick, we take a pill or see a doctor.

Of course, we differ considerably on what makes us feel good. A hungry New Yorker, for instance, might want a hamburger and french fries. A hungry Californian, on the other hand, might opt for a bowl of spicy chili. A dish of carrots and spinach might be completely satisfying to a vegetarian, but dull fare for the gourmet. So that, while a plain loaf of bread will soften the pangs of hunger, we would get much more satisfaction out of eating something we really enjoy. Merchants know this, of course, and provide an endless list of things that will meet our individual needs.

Fun and Excitement

Let's face it, life would be pretty dull without some fun and excitement, and most of us are quite willing to spend our money to obtain a fair share of each. Many Americans strive to excel in sports, and this has created a tremendous market for all types of sporting goods. Others are content to sit on the sidelines and watch, and the sale of tickets for such sports as professional football and ice hockey is increasing steadily. In fact, it is almost impossible to get tickets for games—in some cases, they are sold out before the season even begins!

With more leisure time, Americans are always seeking new and better kinds of entertainment. We buy big color television sets, expensive stereo systems, and error-proof cameras. We go to concerts, plays, and movies and take up interesting new hobbies. We buy vacation homes and campers or travel to the far corners of the world. Our desire for fun and excitement is increasing annually and, as businessmen know, we are spending a great deal of money to satisfy it.

Comfort and Safety

We are also motivated by the desire for comfort and safety. We like shoes that cushion our feet, clothes in which we can move freely, and air conditioners during the hot days of summer. Within recent years many manufacturers have built their businesses on satisfying these desires.

Closely allied to things that simply make us comfortable are labor-saving devices. Since work usually involves a certain amount of effort and exertion, any machine that makes our work load easier increases our sense of comfort. The automatic transmission on a car saves us the effort of shifting gears, for example. Power lawn mowers have lightened the chore of cutting the grass. There seems to be no end to the invention of labor-saving devices. Automatic washers, dryers, dishwashers, knife sharpeners, polishers, even electrically operated toothbrushes, save us effort—and cost us money.

Among the products and services related to safety and comfort are those that allay our fears. We are afraid of being injured, for example, so we are in the market for seat belts, nonskid tires, safety helmets, and fire extinguishers. We naturally dread pain, so we want Novocain when the dentist works on our teeth or aspirin when we have a headache. We are afraid that people will not accept us, so we use mouthwashes and deodorants to avoid giving offense. This understandable desire to feel safe wherever we are is a powerful motive to buy—and we are constantly responding to it.

Love and Approval

It is only natural for us to want certain people to love us or, at least, approve of us. Life, after all, would be very empty without friendship and love—imagine living in an atmosphere of constant disapproval and dislike.

This desire for love and approval motivates us to buy things that we hope will make us more attractive to the people with whom we come in contact. Teen-age girls, for example, buy nearly one-third of the cosmetics sold. Teen-age boys are spending more and more on grooming aids. The aim of both groups, of course, is to enhance their looks. For the same reason, teen-agers buy the kind of clothes that they

One purchase may be the result of a number of motives. Desire for fun and excitement, for love and approval, and for status may all play a role in this decision.

think will attract favorable attention, to say nothing of sighs of envy, from their friends.

Our desire for love and approval motivates us to buy not only for ourselves, but also for other people. We spend money to entertain people we like, and we buy presents for people we love or want to impress. We hope the things we do for them will make them like us all the more.

Self-Realization and Self-Development

When we are children, we are inclined to accept ourselves as we are, just as we take for granted the world in which we live. As we grow older, however, we find that there are many things that we do not know, many ways in which we would like to develop. The desire for *self-development* leads us to find ways to increase our knowledge, talents, and abilities. We want to be smarter, better looking, more poised, and more confident. We want to be able to do things we could not do before. All this leads to a strong desire to develop more fully as individuals and as personalities.

This desire to improve ourselves explains why we spend money on charm or public speaking courses; why we take tennis or karate lessons; why we make attempts to be unique and "do our own thing"—to increase our knowledge, our talents, and our abilities. A girl who invests in a good grooming course will pay not only for that course, but also for cosmetics, hair stylings, and clothes; a girl who takes up tennis will be in the market for rackets, presses, the right tennis outfits, and so on. Generally, however, the money invested in self-development is money well spent.

Self-Image and Status

We all tend to have certain *self-images*—the most attractive girl in the class, the biggest swinger in town, the most sophisticated couple on the block. Unfortunately, that image may be more wishful thinking than reality, so we spend money trying to live up to the goals we have set for ourselves. A boy may spend all of his allowance on clothes. A girl will boast that she goes to all the places the swingers go. A couple will attend plays, concerts, and lectures so that they can impress others with their knowledge of cultural affairs.

Frequently, too, our self-images are ordained by the people with whom we associate. Undoubtedly you have heard the term "keeping up with the Joneses," in many cases an accurate description of a familiar situation. Some people see Bob Jones in a new car and Susie Jones in an expensive fur coat, and since they consider themselves as good as the Joneses—if not better—they must have something as good. Living up to one's self-image can be a very expensive undertaking. Living up to the Joneses can be an even more expensive one.

Impulse Buying

From time to time, even the smartest shoppers give in to the urge to purchase items they had not planned to buy before they entered the store. This is known as *impulse buying*. Consumers may start out intending to buy a specific item. Then, as they go through the various departments in a store or through the aisles in a supermarket, their eyes are caught by something else—a display of "taste-tantalizing snacks" in the supermarket, for instance, or a "fantastic bargain" in an appliance store. They stop, look, and buy—often something that they neither need nor really want.

Merchants are well aware of this urge to buy on impulse. That is why they display attractive, higher-profit items where they can be seen easily. The next time you go shopping, take note of the items you spot first. Chances are, they will not be everyday, routine necessities, such as flour and sugar or socks and underwear. Rather, they will be the more intriguing items, such as frozen pizza and cashmere sweaters—and, your interest caught, you may even give in and buy them.

Compulsive Spending

There are times when we buy because we feel that we have to spend money for "something." We are not always sure what that thing is. This impulse is known as *compulsive spending*. All we know is that by going out and buying something, we will feel better, happier, more at peace with the world.

There are some people who give in to this urge for compulsive spending frequently. There are others, however, who become compulsive spenders only when they are upset, unhappy, or out of sorts with family and friends. They rush out and buy a new sweater, a new belt, or three new lipsticks—and, for some reason, they really do feel better. Needless to say, compulsive spenders are a merchant's delight!

PSYCHOLOGY AND ADVERTISING

It is true that advertising is important to our economy. It helps to broaden our markets and bring down prices. However, consumers need to be able to discern the difference between what is helpful and what is merely a promotional device. To do this, they need some knowledge of just how advertisers see them and how they decide to reach them.

Advertising, of course, tries first to get the consumer's attention, then to move him to buy. It also provides him with information.

However, wise consumers learn to see through the attention-getting devices and look for the facts. And it is on these facts that they base their decisions to buy or not to buy.

Not surprisingly, advertisers spend a great deal of money to find out what makes buyers behave as they do. The reason for this is obvious. Once an advertiser understands what motivates people, he can use this knowledge to sell his goods. Researchers have found that just about every experience we have had leaves an impression on us; it "conditions" us to behave as we do. When an advertisement or commercial ties in with our experiences, we are frequently motivated to buy what is being advertised.

There is a whole field of special study known as "consumer behavior," the study of "what makes people tick"—what motivates people to buy. Of course, sometimes we do not understand ourselves: We do not know why we do one thing, why we do not do another. So psychologists are hired to explore our motives and to dig beneath the surface of our minds to discover those things that we do not know about ourselves.

The field of consumer behavior research, now a billion dollar-a-year business, looks for hidden hopes and dreams, for deep-seated fears and anxieties. Advertisers consider what the researchers have found and use it as a basis for their campaigns. The result is that, rather than selling us "products" as such, advertisers are selling us feelings and dreams. An insurance company, for example, stresses family protection, rather than details about a specific policy. The telephone company emphasizes that you can talk to your loved ones within seconds of dialing the phone. And a car is advertised not only as a means of transportation, but also as a 400-horsepower ego-builder.

HOW ADVERTISERS REACH BUYERS

Advertisers are well aware of the basic needs we discussed previously—those needs for physical well-being, safety, comfort, approval, and so on. Therefore, they do their best to show us how the products they are selling meet these needs in some special way. They use association and suggestion. They appeal to our desire to be different, just as they appeal to our wish to be like everyone else. They remind us that we want to be considered attractive, that we like to get a bargain. And what they are selling, therefore, must be exactly what we want.

Conformity

One of the basic ways that advertisers try to reach us is through their appeal to *conformity*—that is, our inclination to do what our friends do. In teen-agers, of course, this inclination is often very strong. This is understandable, because they are still unsure of their individual talents, abilities, and personalities. But, to a great extent, this inclination to be just like everyone else is also true of adults. Thus we have groups ranging all the way from the "jet set" to the retirement community, members of which can be sold goods and services as the "in thing" for their group. Travel agents conduct tours for people of the same tastes; real estate developers plan housing projects specifically for the elderly, "young marrieds," "swinging singles," and so on; teachers' associations, labor unions, farmers' organizations, all cater to the desire to belong.

The fact is that many of us are uncomfortable if we are considered different; therefore, we tend to do what others do. For example, while we may grumble about the expense of buying new clothes in this year's styles, few of us are individualistic enough to wear something that is out of date—something that we feel we might be laughed at for wearing.

We all want to be in fashion and to be aware of what is really going on. Yet nothing is more fickle than fashion, in clothes or anything else. What is in today may be out tomorrow. Advertisers use this important bit of information to persuade us to buy something new, not because the old has worn out, but because it is no longer in fashion.

Advertisers understand that people want to be like other people—but they also want to be unique. In the ad shown here, the coat has a classic style that appeals to people's desire to dress like other people. However, the description of the coat appeals to the desire for exclusiveness—to be different.

Psychology, Values, and Decision Making   11

Individuality

Although we have a strong desire to do things the way everyone else does, we also have a yearning to be recognized as individuals, people with certain unique qualities and abilities—thus advertisers often appeal to our *individuality*. We feel that we are just a little bit different, a little bit better and smarter than other people. For this reason, advertisements appealing to the "man of distinction" or the "gracious hostess" often disarm us. Similarly, an advertisement that appeals to our superior reasoning powers flatters us. After all, aren't we intelligent, cool, thoughtful consumers? This desire to be a little better than our friends and neighbors may not be our best instinct, but it is a very human one. Millions of dollars worth of cars, jewelry, clothing and other goods are sold to people who want to satisfy this desire to be thought different from everybody else.

Association

When advertisers link a product to people or ideas that will evoke a favorable response, they are appealing to the consumer through *association*. A single idea tends to produce other related ideas, so if the object we are thinking of is pleasant, we tend to have a favorable response to the things we relate to that object. For example, a boy who is an ardent football fan and admires a certain player may be tempted to buy the same kind of clothing his hero wears, drive the type of car he drives or eat the kind of breakfast food he eats. Similarly, a girl might want to purchase the same perfume that is used by a movie star she admires, possibly in the hope that this will make her attractive too. Advertisers, therefore, try to link the product they are selling with people and ideas that can motivate us to buy the product itself.

Suggestion

We all are affected by appeals to emotion or imagination. Although we may not be tempted to contribute to a relief drive for millions of hungry people, the picture of one of them—a crying child—can make us open our wallets. A picture of two happy lovers strolling on the sand of a tropical island is more apt to move us to buy a travel ticket than a page of facts about the island. What we are doing, of course, is identifying ourselves with the couple in the photograph.

Advertisers understand the powerful effect of emotion and imagination. That is why they use *suggestion*—why they try to picture in their ads situations with which we can identify—happy situations, to make us feel that if we buy the product we will find ourselves "in the picture" or unhappy situations that convince us to purchase the product so we can avoid or correct the problem illustrated.

Desire for a Bargain

We all like to think that we are smart shoppers. Indeed, in each of us there may be a small streak of greed, carrying with it the wish to get something for less than it is actually worth, or less than other people paid for it. Advertisers understand this greedy streak only too well, and that is why promotional devices are so effective. The sight of a package, marked with the magic words, "8 cents off," is a powerful incentive to buy even though the words themselves may be meaningless. Eight cents off what? Is the product really being offered at 8 cents less than you would usually pay for it? Or was the product marked up first? It is true that you can find some real bargains in the marketplace, but all too often the "bargain" may cost you more than it is actually worth.

Interest in Sex

We do not have to look far to see how advertisers use our interest in sex to sell goods: Pretty girls, not details about engines, sell cars; attractive waitresses, not raves about the food and drink, are often the reasons for

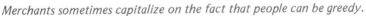

Merchants sometimes capitalize on the fact that people can be greedy.

patronizing a certain restaurant or club; and it is not the high quality of the soap, but the admiring glances of a beautiful woman that help merchandise brand X shaving cream.

Perfume is labeled as "irresistible," an evening dress is called "sexy," lipstick is termed "attention-getting" and "kissable." For the woman who wants men to think her attractive, appeals like these are difficult to resist. Equally difficult for men to resist are products that seem to promise instant success with women. "You'll have a hard time getting away from them," an ad for a toothpaste might warn. And indeed the handsome young man in the commercial is besieged by a horde of beautiful women. What man would not like to be in a similar predicament?

Youth

There are millions of young people between the ages of 13 and 17 in the United States—and these teen-agers have many billions of dollars in earnings, allowances, and family loans to spend as they wish.

Not only are teen-agers important because they have money to spend; equally important is their influence on the market. Today the emphasis is on looking and feeling young. What young people wear, what they say, how they act, and what they purchase, influence the buying habits of adults.

Naturally, business is always ready to cash in on a growing market. The teen-ager, who has always been a good buyer of things like records, radios, and movies, is proving an equally good customer for other items. Banks cater to teen-agers, a large number of whom now have charge accounts. Stores set aside departments especially planned to sell teen-age merchandise. Even investment firms are getting into the act—there are now over a million young stockholders.

Car manufacturers are employing racing car drivers and mechanics to conduct clinics on "souping up" cars. Not only are these clinics an opportunity for the sale of customized accessories, but also they make teen-agers brand conscious in their future purchase of an automobile. In addition, the sale of products that make girls more attractive to boys—and vice versa—is certainly big business. Teen-agers spend millions of dollars on cosmetics and grooming aids; and some of these must work, because sales to prospective brides are booming—the market for home furnishings and appliances, for example is a thriving one.

PROMOTIONAL DEVICES AND SCHEMES

In order to sell his merchandise, to say nothing of making a profit, the merchant first has to attract the customer's attention and then move the customer to action—that is, get him to buy the product. One way of doing this is by using psychology in planning ads. Another way is using promotional devices—sales, come-ons, discounts, contests, and the like—to get us to open our wallets and buy.

Sales

We have discussed the fact that we all like to get a bargain. That is one reason why the word "sale" rarely fails to attract our attention. Happily, we think that we may be able to buy a product at less than its usual cost—and, many times, this is possible. No merchant wants to have his money tied up in merchandise that is simply gathering dust on a shelf. He wants to get rid of his stock, turning it into money with which he can buy newer or fresher products. It is better, therefore, to put slow-moving merchandise on sale, even though his profits on the sale will be much lower than he would like.

Therefore, there are many legitimate sales put on by good stores and reputable merchants. Many of these are seasonal sales; they are held at times of the year when the merchandise would not normally be selling well.

If you are willing to wait for such sales, setting aside the money to buy the items you want, you can get some genuine bargains. A new car of the current model, for example, can usually be purchased just before a newer model is introduced at a saving of $300 or more. Winter clothes are put on sale the day after Christmas, summer clothes in mid-July, and air conditioners in February. Christmas cards, ornaments, and wrappings can be bought at about half their regular price after Christmas.

Seasonal sales are not the only kind to be held. Merchants often hold special sales to market their products. Among them are:

- *Penny Sales.* One item is sold at the regular price and another of the same kind costs only a penny more.
- *Dollar Sales.* Some items are priced at $1, but they are usually grouped with other items for which you must pay $3 to $5 more.
- *Odds and Ends Sales.* All unsold merchandise is lumped together so that the merchant can clear his shelves.
- *Inventory Sales.* Just before or just after taking stock, the merchant attempts to move all unsold goods.
- *Special Event Sales.* To capitalize on the fact that people spend more freely at certain times, the merchant holds Christmas, Easter, Back-to-School, and other special event sales.

The important thing to remember about sales is that, unless you are shrewd enough to know your own needs and to recognize real values, you can load yourself up with bad buys. Price is only one thing to consider when buying at sales; the most important thing is value. No matter how cheap an article is, it is not a bargain if you cannot use it, if the quality is poor, if you have no place to store it, if it deteriorates before you can use it, or if you buy more than you really need.

Come-Ons

In an effort to meet competition and increase sales, merchants sometimes use gimmicks, or *come-ons,* which are designed to make us think we are getting something for nothing, or at least at very substantial savings.

One of the most common come-ons is the *loss leader.* This is a product that a merchant will offer at the wholesale price, or at even less than he actually paid for it, in order to attract customers to the store in the hope that they will buy other items at the same time. Generally, the loss leader will be placed near the rear of the store. As customers go down the aisles to get to the great bargain, they see all sorts of attractive, more expensive items that appeal to them. If people buy enough of these impulse items, the merchant will more than make up for the lack of any profit on the loss leader.

Discounts

One of the merchant's favorite ways to encourage buying is to offer a *discount*—that is, an opportunity to purchase something at less than the regular price. In some cases, these discounts represent real savings. In others, however, the merchant has first marked up the original retail price, so there is no real saving involved. This type of discount should not be confused with discounts of 2 percent or more for prompt payment of bills, or for immediate payment in cash, which usually represent real savings.

Something for Nothing

Merchants use all sorts of promotional devices to put people in a buying mood. We may be given "free" coupons to introduce us to a new product, offered a "free" dinner for trying out new cookware, loaded down with "free" flash bulbs when buying an expensive camera. And gas stations, like other merchants, often run contests or provide "free" gifts when we buy a certain quantity of gas.

One of the most popular and widespread promotional devices, of course, is giving trading stamps at the time a purchase is made. With these stamps, we are told, we can get "free" merchandise, and an

Consumers never really get "something for nothing."

attractive catalogue that displays these wonderful gifts is always available. Since the usual cash value of a trading stamp is 1/10 of a cent, hundreds or even thousands of stamps must be saved in order to get anything of value. However, the shopper cannot afford not to save the stamps, since the price of the merchandise they acquire with stamps has already been added to the cost of items bought.

It is important to remember that no product or service is really free. No merchant can afford to give away anything of value, without making up the cost somewhere else. Thus all prizes, contests, and giveaways must be paid for in some way—by the consumer. Most authorities estimate that such sales promotion devices add from 1 to 5 percent to the cost of the goods sold.

Easy Credit

Easy credit, the "buy now and pay later" approach, can be a very strong inducement in getting people to buy more and more frequently. "No down payment . . . easy terms . . . 36 months to pay!" the ads proclaim, "so why do without things that you'd really like to have?"

It all sounds so easy that many people are lured into the trap. True, there are times when buying on credit is necessary and legitimate. But the cost of credit is high; you may be paying an annual rate of 18 percent interest on your department store bills, for example. And by buying everything you want immediately, simply because you do not have to pay for it now, you may be on the way to a debt-ridden future.

1 What is the purpose of consumer education?

2 How does a consumer vote for the continued production of a particular product or service?

3 Who decides what articles are to be produced for sale in the United States?

4 What influences determine our attitudes and opinions toward those things that seem most important to us?

5 How do our personal values determine the ways in which we spend our money?

6 List seven forces that motivate us to buy goods and services.

7 How does our desire for fun and excitement influence the ways we spend our money?

8 Name some items people commonly purchase because of their desire to be comfortable and safe.

9 What is the meaning of the expression, "keeping up with the Joneses"?

10 What causes some individuals to become compulsive spenders?

11 Why do advertisers hire psychologists to study consumer behavior?

12 List six appeals advertisers commonly use to influence consumers to buy their merchandise.

13 What are some promotional devices merchants use to get consumers to buy their products?

14 Why are loss leaders usually placed in the rear of a store?

15 Is it true that discounts in merchandise always represent real savings for a consumer? Why or why not?

16 In what way is the availability of easy credit often a problem for the consumer?

CONSUMER PROBLEMS AND PROJECTS

1 Write a short autobiography in which you tell about yourself and about those values you believe are the most important. Indicate how your values affect the ways you spend your money. Show your autobiography to your parents and ask them to tell you whether they agree or disagree with your attitudes and opinions. Then add a paragraph to what you have already written in which you point out how your values differ from those of your parents. When you have completed your composition, discuss the contents with your parents.

2 Watch a number of television commercials and note three that appeal to the viewer's hidden hopes and dreams or his fears and anxieties. Report to the class what you have discovered in your analysis of these commercials.

3 Visit a supermarket in your community and draw a rough floor plan showing the layout of the store. On your plan indicate what types of items are placed to the right of the entrance, in the aisles, at the back of the store, and near the cash register. Also note on your plan where loss leaders or "specials" are displayed. Then write a short report in which you indicate why the supermarket manager located the items in the places where you found them.

4 Make a survey of the makes and models of automobiles owned by families living in your neighborhood. (If you live in an area where most people do not own cars, substitute another product, such as television sets.) Note especially the makes and models owned by families with only one car and the makes and models owned by those families with two or more cars. On the basis of your survey, answer the following questions: (a) Do you find evidence that car owners in your neighborhood follow the practice of "keeping up with the Joneses"? (b) Are expensive luxury models found in your neighborhood? Why or why not? (c) If a family owns two or more cars, do they tend to be of about equal value? Give reasons for your answers.

5 Prepare a scrapbook in which you include ads from well-known magazines. Include advertisements that use the following appeals: (a) conformity, (b) association, (c) suggestion, (d) desire for individuality, (e) attractiveness to the opposite sex. Under each ad write a sentence identifying the specific appeal it represents. Recent issues of popular magazines, such as *Sports Illustrated, Newsweek, McCall's,* and *Good Housekeeping,* should contain ads you might clip for this project.

6 Select at least five food products that are being promoted as "cents-off" specials at a store in your community. Check prices of the items you have chosen in a supermarket or discount store. Figure the actual amount the consumer pays when he uses a cents-off coupon. Also ask the store manager to tell you the price quoted for each item before it was advertised as a cents-off special. Record the information you have gathered in a table using the headings shown below. After you have completed your table, write a paragraph indicating whether or not you think cents-off promotions represent real savings to the consumer.

Name of Product	Price Before Special Was Announced	Shelf Price	Number of Cents Off	Actual Price

Effective Consumer Behavior

Some people have described the marketplace in which we buy goods and services as a jungle, but the market is not quite as bad as that. Perhaps a better definition would be that it is like a fair, with hundreds of people trying to sell us thousands of things. Some of these are things we need; others are things we want; still others are things we can be made to want, even though we have no real need for them. With so much to choose from, therefore, deciding what to buy can be very difficult.

CONSUMER BUYING SKILLS

How can we go through this marketplace and get a reasonable amount of satisfaction from the money we spend? Well, we have already learned something about how the market operates, how manufacturers produce a wide variety of goods and services, and how they try to persuade us to buy them. The next step is to consider some of the guidelines that can help us to make wise buying decisions. These guidelines include such things as planning ahead, finding the best places to shop for different kinds of products, and learning how to use the helpful signposts that can guide us through the maze of the marketplace. Even with these guidelines our shopping trips will not always be without problems and disappointments. A certain number of these beset even the smartest shoppers. However, it is comforting to know there are people and organizations that can provide us with further help—both in making us better-informed consumers and in protecting us from those unscrupulous producers and sellers who sometimes prey upon us.

Plan Your Buying

Spending money wisely is really an art, one that is certainly worth developing. Although it will not increase the amount of money you have, wise spending can increase the amount of goods and services you can buy with that money. Furthermore, it can help you get greater satisfaction from the money you do spend.

The first step in learning to buy more wisely is to plan ahead. Unfortunately, it is a step that many people overlook. They take whatever money they have and spend it on anything that catches their fancy. By buying in this impulsive manner, they frequently waste money on items they do not need or cannot really use; and they may have to do without things they should have because they have no money left with which to buy them.

By planning ahead, however, you can avoid many buying mistakes; you can then use your money for the things you really need and want. This kind of planning involves determining what you need now and what you would like to have in the future and knowing what and when to buy to get the best and most for your money.

Short-Range Planning   The things you need for the next few days and weeks are the things you will have to plan for first. You may need money for food and carfare, for example. You may need to have shoes repaired or clothes cleaned. You may have to buy a birthday gift for a friend or a new outfit for a party you are going to next weekend. These immediate needs must be met before you can think about the things you might like to have later on.

In carefully considering your immediate needs, you may find that some of them can be modified or put off. Instead of buying a birthday gift, you may decide that you can make something for your friend—a batch of his favorite cookies, perhaps, or a unique suede belt. Or you may decide that you really do not need a new outfit for that party after all. The clothes that you already have will do perfectly well. Then the money that you do not spend now can be set aside for something that you would like in the future.

When deciding what to buy now remember to take advantage of seasonal bargains. From a financial standpoint, there is a best time to buy just about everything, this "best time" being the weeks or months when you can get the most value for the money you spend. Products purchased at such times are known as *seasonal bargains.* Fresh fruits and vegetables, for example, are cheapest (and most delicious) when they are in season. Beef, lamb, poultry, and eggs are better buys at certain times of the year. Winter coats are an especially good buy in August, air conditioners in February, and household linens in January.

Learn to buy according to the calendar. Watch for newspaper advertisements and radio and television commercials announcing seasonal sales. Taking note of just when stores in your locality seem to feature certain products is one way to ensure that your dollars will stretch to cover more of the things you want or need.

Before starting out on a shopping trip be sure to make a shopping list. Starting off on a shopping expedition without making a list first

A good shopping list starts with the essentials.

can be a risky venture. For one thing, you may not remember all the items you intended to buy; for another, you may be more easily tempted to buy other things you do not need or cannot afford.

It is a good idea, therefore, to make out a shopping list before every shopping trip; unless, of course, it is simply a hurried dash to pick up the salt you forgot to buy the first time. List the items you want to buy in the light of the money you have to spend—with the things you must buy first, the less essential items at the end. In this way you will be sure to have enough money for the things you really need; you can add other items as your pocketbook allows.

Long-Range Planning   Most of us are not millionaires; nor do we have some rich relative who would be only too happy to pay all our bills. The result is that, while we can usually provide for our daily living expenses, we sometimes find that we do not have enough money for some of the more expensive items that we will need or want in the months and years ahead.

The first step in long-range planning, then, is to assess, as closely as possible, your plans for the future. What will you be doing? Where will you be going? What changes will you be making? What will you need money for? A new winter coat, for example, or a long series of dental treatments? A camping trip this summer or college tuition next fall? Many of these future needs may involve large expenditures of money; the next step, therefore, is to determine how you can get it.

Can you set aside a certain amount from your weekly income, perhaps cutting down on nonessentials in order to save more? Or can you count on receiving extra funds at specific times—from a Christmas club account or a regular bonus, for example? Can these be earmarked for future needs? Or perhaps you should get a part-time job so that you can earn enough money to meet particularly heavy expenses?

As you estimate the number of things you will need and their costs, you may find that you have to stretch your buying plans over several years. This may seem like a long time to wait for some of the things you want, but it is the only sure way of avoiding financial headaches and attaining things of real value.

Be a Comparison Shopper

If every merchant sold the same products at the same prices as his competitors, it might not make too much difference where you shopped. This is not the case, however. All stores do not offer the same products, or the same quality of goods, at the same prices. There are several reasons for this.

A large department store, for example, may provide a great many services for its customers: charge accounts, free delivery of purchases, free alterations, and the like. These services add to the store's operating costs; the store must charge more for the products it sells in order to cover the costs and make a profit. A chain or a discount store, on the other hand, may provide few customer services if any; with the resulting lower operating costs, a discount store can usually afford to sell its merchandise at lower prices. Also, some merchants are satisfied with a reasonable profit. Others are out to get every last penny they can.

Smart shoppers, therefore, do not shop at only one store; they do *comparison shopping* by visiting a number of stores and comparing quality, services, and prices. Then they make their purchases at those stores that offer good value at a price they can afford.

Know Your Merchant

Certainly, you would not want to buy anything from someone who was trying to cheat you; nor would you want to shop in a store where the salespeople were constantly pressuring you to buy and where there was no chance of getting your money back if you were not satisfied with what you had bought. Unfortunately, there are some merchants who are dishonest, some stores that are run on a who-cares-about-the-customer basis. It is wise to avoid them whenever possible.

Instead, buy from reputable merchants who believe in treating their customers fairly. They will be helpful rather than pushy, informative rather than indifferent. They will also stand behind the merchandise they sell. Should anything be wrong with something you have bought, they will willingly exchange it or repair it or refund your money. After all, they want you to be satisfied with your purchase, because if you are, you will probably buy from them again.

Know Your Merchandise

It is astonishing that so many people really know very little about what they are buying. They buy haphazardly, attracted by a color or a style, a package or a low price. And they seem unconcerned about whether a particular item is really worth buying or whether it actually meets their needs.

The fact is that the more you know about the things you buy, the more likely you are to buy wisely. For this reason, it is smart to inspect all potential purchases carefully. Examine them inside and out; check even the smallest details. Most important, read the labels to find out what the manufacturer has to say about the product. It is only when you know what a product contains, how it is made, and how it should be used that you can really determine whether it meets your needs.

Labels   The labels and tags found on many products are actually messages about those products. *Labels* tell you something about what you will be getting if you purchase the products.

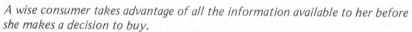

A wise consumer takes advantage of all the information available to her before she makes a decision to buy.

The label on a sweater, for example, might indicate the name of the manufacturer or distributor; what the sweater is made of (100 percent wool); how it will perform (it will resist stains and pilling); and how it should be cared for (wash in cool water, using mild soap). The tag on a television set might indicate the manufacturer, the size of the screen, and specific instructions about aerials and cables. The label on a can of stew might list such things as the ingredients in the stew (in descending order, according to volume); whether it contains artificial coloring, flavoring, or chemical preservatives; how it should be prepared; and, of course, the name of the company that distributes it.

Unfortunately, not all products carry labels and tags with sufficient information. Learn to look for those that do, and read the labels carefully before you buy, particularly if the product is one that you have not tried before—this can make the difference between wise and foolish buying.

Grades When you buy food, you naturally want to get good quality—and you want to get the quality you paid for. To help you do just that, the U.S. Department of Agriculture has established *grades*, or quality standards, for a number of foods. Beef, for example, is graded as Prime (the best), Choice, Good, Standard, and Commercial. Milk and cream are graded A, B, and C. Processed (canned, dried, and frozen) fruits and vegetables have grade names such as U.S. Grade A or U.S. Fancy, U.S. Grade B or U.S. Choice, U.S. Grade C or U.S. Standard. Some food items will have the grade listed on the label or package, but others may not. With fruits and vegetables in particular, you may have to make your choice on the basis of brand names. Each brand stands for a certain quality. If you become familiar with different brands, you can determine the quality represented by each.

It is not always necessary to buy the top grades. The lower grades of a particular product may be just as nutritious, just as good to eat. And of course, they are less expensive.

Look for Guarantees and Warranties

To all intents and purposes, a *guarantee* and a warranty are the same thing. Basically, they are a promise to the consumer that he will be compensated in some way if the product he buys does not perform the way it should. It is important to note, however, that a guarantee, no matter how sincerely it is worded, is worthless unless the company issuing it honestly wishes to satisfy its customers. Many companies, of course, stand behind the products they make. Depending on the circumstances, they will replace or repair a product that is defective—or even refund the purchase price. There are other firms, though, that promise a great deal and deliver nothing.

A guarantee is particularly important when you are considering the purchase of expensive items, such as color television sets, refrigerators, and automobiles. Remember, however, that the single word "guaranteed" on a product means nothing. It is only when the guarantee explicitly states what is guaranteed, for how long, and under what terms, that it has any meaning and value. Only the picture tube in a television set might be covered by the guarantee, for example, or only the heating unit in a steam iron. If any other parts of these products prove to be defective, it is up to you to pay for the replacements and repairs.

Naturally, it is wise to buy the products of manufacturers who have reputations for dealing fairly with their customers. But fairness is a two-way street. Responsible consumers handle products carefully and use them in the way they were meant to be used. If something does go wrong with a product, they can honestly say it was not their fault, and they have the right to expect fair treatment from the manufacturer of that product.

Check Conditions of Sale

Have you ever had an experience like this? You buy a shirt you really like at a sale. When you get home and take a closer look at your great bargain, you see that there is a big stain on one sleeve. Disheartened, you try to return your purchase, but the store issues a firm, "No." The sale, it turns out, was a *final sale*—no exchanges, no refunds—a fact that you had not noticed in your excitement over your fabulous buy.

Smart consumers learn to take nothing on faith. They check everything before they buy, posing questions like these:

- Can a product be exchanged for a similar one in another size or color?
- Within what time limits must such an exchange be made?
- If a particular item is returned, will the merchant issue a cash refund or a store credit?
- Is a service contract or a service warranty included with a particular product?
- Under what circumstances will a defective product be repaired or replaced?
- Is the sale a final one?

If they are buying on credit, they ask questions like these:

- What is the exact rate of interest?
- How and when must installment payments be made?
- What happens if installment payments are late?

A wise consumer checks the conditions of sale before he buys.

CONSUMER HELP AND INFORMATION

We have just described some of the guidelines that can help us to make better buying decisions. But do you now have enough information to go into the marketplace and make the best possible choice every time you buy something? Probably not. If you want the best piece of meat for your money, for example, you would not have any problem selecting it—you could simply choose the one marked U.S. Prime. But suppose you are faced with twelve different television sets, all sold at about the same price, all with exactly the same guarantees and the same conditions of sale? Which one should you buy? Which one would provide the best picture, the clearest sound? Which would prove the most durable? Does one set have safety features that another does not? Is one manufacturer more reliable than another?

Where can you find answers to questions like these? Happily, for you and your fellow consumers, you can get information from a number of sources: from consumer testing agencies, for example, and trade associations and magazines; from federal, state, and local government agencies; from your local library; even from your own relatives and friends.

The Experiences of Others

If you wanted to know whether or not a movie was worth seeing, you would consult a friend who had seen it. If you wanted to find out whether a party had been a swinging success or a complete bore, you would ask someone who had been there. Why not, then, use your friends and relatives as a source of information when you are puzzled about just what to buy? Their praise or criticism of a particular product can give you at least some indication of its worth.

It is important, however, that you do not judge a product simply on the opinions of others. The poor performance of your cousin's television set may be due to the fact that he does not know how to tune it properly; your best friend's "fantastic" jeans may not be subjected to the hard wear you would give them. It is fine to ask people for their opinions, but you should consult more objective sources, too. When you use such sources, you have a better chance of making the right buying decision.

Popular Literature

Consumer affairs, consumer interests, consumer education, consumer protection—all of these issues are news these days. It is almost impossible to pick up a newspaper and not find at least one article relating to the consumer. And the same holds true for the family service magazines like *The Ladies Home Journal* and *McCall's.* Both newspapers and magazines cover a wide range of topics—and provide a great deal of useful information.

One particular magazine, *Changing Times,* has become primarily a magazine for consumers. The majority of articles appearing in it deal with subjects like budgeting, home building, credit, and insurance; they are to the point and, on the whole, completely objective. One reason for this is that *Changing Times*, like *Consumer Reports* and *Consumers' Research* Magazine, accepts no advertisements. It can state the facts, without fear of any financial pressure from advertisers. This is not true, of course, of many other publications.

Undoubtedly, your local library will have a number of books on consumer-related subjects. It will also have many of the magazines that consistently carry articles on consumer issues and consumer affairs. If you are truly interested in becoming a smart consumer, you will learn to take advantage of the resources your own library offers.

Consumer Testing Agencies

Many of the products that are offered for sale in the marketplace have been tested by one or more *consumer testing agency.* The written reports that give the results of these tests can provide much useful information about products you are thinking of buying.

Large department and chain stores, like Macy's, Sears Roebuck, Montgomery Ward, and J.C. Penney, have specific programs for testing and grading the products they sell. There are also commercial testing laboratories. For a fee, they will test sample products supplied by manufacturers, who, in turn, may use the results of the tests in their advertisements. Naturally, they might not include any critical comments—"irritating hum when the radio is tuned above a certain sound level," for instance, or "lock tends to spring open at the slightest touch." After all, their aim is to present a favorable report on their product. Still, whatever information is given can be used in shaping your buying decisions.

Consumers' Research, Inc., and Consumers Union of U.S., Inc. are run on a different basis. Both of these organizations buy products in the open market and run them through a series of tests to judge their performance, serviceability, and comparative worth. In their reports, they point out the faults as well as the good qualities of all the products they test, and the results of their tests may not be used in advertisements.

Consumers' Research publishes its reports in the *Consumers' Research* and a *Consumer Bulletin Annual*. Consumers Union reports in *Consumer Reports* and its Annual *Buying Guide*. These periodicals are available in most libraries, or you can subscribe to them on an annual basis—the subscription fees are reasonable.

Seals of Approval

Certain associations issue *seals of approval* to products that have met their standards; these seals are placed on the merchandise, and they tell you something about the quality of a product. Appliances bearing the Underwriters' Laboratory Seal of Approval, for example, have been judged safe electrically. Furniture bearing the Seal of Integrity, issued by the National Association of Furniture Manufacturers, is guaranteed "free from any defects in workmanship, material, and construction for a reasonable time, but not less than 12 months after delivery to the customer." Stoves with the seal of the American Gas Association have been judged well-made and safe.

Some family magazines, like *Good Housekeeping, McCall's,* and *Parents',* also award seals of approval to some of the products they have tested in their own laboratories. These can be useful guides in some instances, but since the seals are awarded only to products that are advertised in the magazine, some people question their value.

Other Nongovernment Sources

There are a number of nongovernment sources of consumer information and protection. The *better business bureaus,* for example, are operated on a nonprofit basis by business firms in many communities. Their aims are to maintain advertising and selling practices that are fair to business and consumers alike and to eliminate misrepresentation and trickery in business dealings. The bureaus will give you information about business organizations in your locality and deal with complaints about those firms that use unscrupulous practices. In some communities, the local chamber of commerce, although organized primarily for the promotion of business, indirectly protects consumers as well.

Well aware that they need all the help they can get, consumers are also establishing their own organizations on a voluntary basis. These groups work to promote sound consumer laws that will be effectively enforced, to educate consumers so that they can buy more wisely, and to gather and disseminate information of value to consumers. By banding together, these consumers are fighting their own battles in a most effective manner.

Government Sources

The federal government provides information, not on specific brands and products, but on such things as safety and health standards and hazards. Its various agencies also are becoming more and more involved in consumer protection, as consumer demands and pressures increase. For example:

● The Federal Trade Commission tries to guard against false advertising and fraudulent sales promotion.

Consumers have begun to help themselves through voluntary organizations.
Bruce Anspach/Editorial Photocolor Archives, Inc.

- The Food and Drug Administration tries to protect us against health hazards. With 96,000 manufacturing plants to supervise and a limited staff to do the job, however, this protection is not as complete as it should be.

- The Antitrust Division of the Department of Justice checks on attempts to control the markets for such items as drugs, jewelry, and food products.

- The Department of Agriculture regulates food products that cross boundaries of any one state before they are sold. It establishes grades for many products and inspects others.

- The U.S. Postal Service tries to protect consumers from mail fraud.

The various departments of the federal government also offer the kind of information that can help consumers make better buying decisions. The U.S. Department of Agriculture, for example, publishes more than a hundred bulletins on topics ranging from money management to buying toys. Many of these government bulletins are free; all you have to do is write for them. Others must be purchased, but the cost is usually minimal. To find out exactly what is available, you can contact Consumer Product Information, Public Documents Distribution Center, Pueblo, Colorado 81009.

Increasingly, state governments are becoming involved in consumer affairs. Through special agencies and publicly supported colleges, they provide information on many topics of interest to consumers. In addition, many states have established some form of consumer-frauds bureau, usually under the aegis of the state attorney general. These bureaus handle consumer complaints about such things as false labeling, selling under false pretenses, and deceptive real estate practices. How successful such a bureau is, of course, depends primarily on just how much power the attorney general has to follow through on complaints.

Some cities and counties have also set up consumer councils and bureaus of consumer affairs. These, too, provide helpful information and handle consumer complaints.

Let the Buyer Beware

With so many available sources of information and help, why do we consumers still have such problems in the marketplace? One reason, of course, is that there are just too many dishonest people, with too many "quick buck" schemes. In spite of all the laws and agencies to protect the consumer, unscrupulous dealers and merchants can still think of ways to cheat the unwary buyer.

There is a more important reason for our problems, however. We frequently do not seek information and help until it is too late. We buy without knowing what we are really buying. We buy from people we know nothing about. Then we are surprised and outraged to find that we have been cheated, that we have wasted our money.

In this less than perfect world, the old saying, *caveat emptor* (Let the buyer beware) still holds true. The smart consumer pays heed to this warning. He gets all the facts he can BEFORE he makes a purchase. He turns to the agencies that can help him BEFORE he signs a contract. He makes sure that he is an informed consumer—and, as a result, he has fewer problems in the marketplace.

CHECKING YOUR READING

1 Why does an effective consumer prepare a plan before he starts to shop?

2 How can you learn to buy according to the calendar?

3 Why does a shopper often make his plans several years in advance?

4 Do all merchants offer the same products or the same quality of products at the same prices? Why or why not?

5 What are the characteristics of a reputable merchant?

6 Is it necessary to always buy the top grades of meats, fruits, and vegetables? Why or why not?

7 For what types of merchandise is a guarantee particularly important?

8 Why do responsible consumers handle the merchandise they purchase with care?

9 What questions does a careful shopper ask before making a decision to buy a particular item?

10 How can relatives and friends help you when you are puzzled about what you should buy? Why should you not rely on these sources entirely?

11 What is the purpose of the local better business bureau?

12 How do the test results reported by Consumers' Research and Consumers Union differ from those provided by other testing agencies?

13 Why do some shoppers question the value of the seals of approval that are issued by family magazines?

14 Name some agencies of the federal government that issue reports on the safety and health standards of goods we buy.

15 What services do state governments often provide to help the consumer?

16 Does the old saying, "Let the buyer beware," still hold true? Why or why not?

1 Suppose you are going to buy some clothes to wear to school. Assume you will need shirts, pants or skirts, socks, underwear, and a pair of shoes. Determine the maximum amount of money you can spend; then check ads in a daily newspaper that circulates in your community and prepare a written short-range shopping plan.

2 Mrs. Schafer always buys sheets and pillow cases in the fall. Mrs. Sanders waits until January and buys these items when white sales are held at many stores. Which woman do you believe is the more effective shopper? Give reasons for your answer.

3 Select five varieties of canned vegetables and compare the shelf prices for which they are being sold at three supermarkets in your community. Try to choose stores owned by three different companies and be sure you select cans that are exactly the same size and, if possible, the same brand for each vegetable in all three stores. Prepare a table with the headings below.

Variety of Vegetable	Brand	Can Size	Shelf Prices		
			Store A	Store B	Store C

Write a short report in which you give reasons for any price differences you found in your survey.

4 Prepare a bulletin board or scrapbook of seals of approval. Clip seals from magazines or draw facsimiles of them. Try to collect seals from as many of the following organizations as you can: American Dental Association, American Gas Association, *Good Housekeeping*, National Association of Furniture Manufacturers, *Parents' Magazine*, Underwriters' Laboratories. Under each seal, mount a picture of a product given the seal of approval; below each picture place a short statement indicating the value of the seal.

5 Assume that you want to purchase a complete stereo system for your room. Obtain a copy of the most recent *Consumer Reports* Annual *Buying Guide* or Consumers' Research *Annual Bulletin*. Determine what the testing agency recommends as the best buy for each of the following stereo components: stereo pickup cartridge, turntable and changer, magnetic tape deck and recorder, stereo receiver, loudspeaker, and headphones. Prepare a report listing the prices of the components you have selected and the total cost of your proposed project. Compare the prices with those at which the components are sold at a well-known store in your community.

3 Consumer Issues

If this world of ours were perfect, we would not have any problems. But, of course, it is not perfect and problems abound. Many of these problems are linked to money: its value is continually decreasing; some people do not have enough, others want too much. Other problems concern the world, our natural and our man-made environment. The landscape is contaminated by soot, gas, dyes, chemicals, ear-shattering noise, and just plain junk. We have not yet found a way to eliminate poverty or crime. All of these problems have become issues that must be considered by consumers; they must be solved if we are going to have a decent world in which to live.

A study of consumer issues and responsibilities should help you to understand some of the bigger problems that touch your life and the lives of others. As a young consumer, you will have an important part to play in deciding just how these problems should be solved.

THE MARKETPLACE

The marketplace in which you do your shopping is indeed like a fair. It is filled with an attractive and tempting array of products; it reverberates with the cries of the merchants who want you to buy what they have to sell. And it is crowded with shoppers who want to buy the things they see only to find out that the money they have is not sufficient. The prices at the fair have become too high.

Prices

When you go shopping, what are the first things you consider? A brand name, an attractive package, a favorite color, the newest style—these are all the things that probably first catch your attention. Then, having found what you want, you look to see how much it costs. Sometimes the price is right; it is one you can afford. At other times, however, the price is all wrong, at least for you. It is well beyond the reach of your limited income.

What determines the price of goods and services? One factor is the amount that people are willing to pay. If toothbrushes are offered for sale at $3 each and nobody buys them, the manufacturer will have to lower his price or go out of business. If, on the other hand, these same toothbrushes become so popular that they are soon in short supply, the manufacturer could raise the price to $5 and still have customers fighting to buy his wares.

Another factor that affects prices is the cost of the materials and labor that were used to produce a specific product. Naturally, the production cost of a hand-made silver cup is going to be far greater than the production cost of a machine-molded plastic cup. And those differences in cost will be reflected in their prices.

A third factor affecting prices is the fact that in certain product categories a small number of companies produce all the products. In this country, for example, a few large companies produce almost all breakfast cereals. Such large producers can and do exert tremendous control over market prices. After all, if you do not choose to buy their products at their prices, what other choice do you have?

In recent years, prices have been steadily rising. So has the cost of producing goods and services. The overall results are lowered productivity and inflation, which force people to spend more and more for the things they need and want.

Inflation

"To inflate" means to swell or distend, to blow up, or to expand abnormally. In economics, *inflation* is an increase (or abnormal expansion) of the amount of money and credit in proportion to the amount of goods available; this increase causes prices to rise. And this is just what has happened to our economy. According to the Bureau of Labor Statistics, between 1950 and 1970 the cost of living rose 61.3 percent. Each year we have been paying more for what we buy, even though the things we purchase are actually not worth any more than they were the year before.

Inflation is like a thief; it robs you of your purchasing power. For example, although a dollar will still buy "a dollar's worth" of breakfast cereals, the amount of cereal you get for that dollar will change. In 1970, $1 would buy only as much cereal as you could have bought for 71 cents in 1955. Your money buys less because its real value has gone down.

If you are lucky enough to have your income rise as prices rise, you may not notice the effects of inflation. But for people who have limited or fixed incomes, the effects can be catastrophic: They still

Because of inflation, the consumer's dollar no longer buys as much as it once did.

have only a small amount of money to spend and, somehow, they must make it go far enough to buy at least the essentials. With prices rising higher and higher, this becomes more and more difficult; and for some people, it soon becomes impossible.

Can anything be done to halt inflation? The government has tried at least to hold down the rate of inflation. Many economists, however, think it is not possible to have economic growth without some inflation. The question then becomes how much? A 3 percent rise in the cost of living every year, which some people would consider acceptable, would mean that prices would be 15 percent higher five years from now.

THE ENVIRONMENT

Ordinarily, when we think of a consumer we think of someone who buys food or clothing, an automobile or a television set; someone who then uses what he has bought. Webster's Seventh New Collegiate Dictionary, however, has some other meanings for the word "consume." Among them are these: "To do away with completely: destroy . . . to spend wastefully: squander . . . to waste or burn away."

Many of the problems we face today stem from the fact that, over the years, we have not been intelligent consumers. Instead, we have "spent wastefully," we have "squandered" our natural resources, we have "destroyed" much of our environment. One reason for this, of course, is that until fairly recently, our natural resources seemed endless. Conservationists and environmentalists now tell us, however, that we have only a few years left, certainly not longer than until the end of this century, in which to change our ways. We must stop polluting the world around us now, in order to save and conserve our natural resources for the future.

Pollution

Of all the problems consumers face, pollution is probably the most critical. *Pollution* is the entering of impure or unclean elements into our environment, making it an unhealthy place to live. It is all very well to use care in buying the things we need and want. But if we are too sick to use the things we have bought, or not around to enjoy them, then all our buying skills will have been of little advantage. Unless we change our ways, this is the situation in which we could find ourselves. Unless we stop polluting the air, for example, we may choke to death on poisonous gases. Unless we use only the safest fertilizers and pesticides, we may poison the very food we eat. Unless we stop polluting our waterways, we may poison ourselves with industrial wastes—and animal and human wastes as well. Unless we find a way to handle solid waste—things such as empty bottles and beer cans, scrapped automobiles and discarded refrigerators—we shall carpet the landscape knee-deep with junk.

In a message to Congress on February 10, 1970, President Nixon emphasized the critical situation that faces us:

Like those in the last century who tilled a plot of land to exhaustion and then moved on to another, we in this century have too casually and too long abused our natural environment. The time has come when we can wait no longer to repair the damage already done, and to establish new criteria to guide us in the future . . .

The tasks that need doing require money, resolve and ingenuity—and they are too big to be done by government alone. They call for fundamentally new philosophies of land, air and water use, for stricter regulation, for expanded government action, for greater citizen involvement, and for new programs to insure that government, industry, and individuals all are called on to do their share of the job and to pay their share of the cost.

As individuals and as consumers, therefore, we must be vitally concerned with all forms of pollution—pollution of our water and air, pollution from noise and solid waste. If we do not take positive steps to end them today, we may find that tomorrow is indeed too late.

Water Pollution   Do you have a favorite place to swim? A cold, deep lake, perhaps, or a wide, meandering river; a sandy ocean beach? Suppose, then, that the next time you wanted to go swimming, you went to that favorite place and saw a new sign: "Swimming prohibited. Water is polluted." You would not like that at all, would you? Neither would anyone else who wanted to swim there. Yet, due to our carelessness, "no swimming" signs are appearing at more and more of the nation's favorite swimming places.

Just how have our waters become so polluted? Well, for one thing, cities and towns dump raw sewage into nearby waterways; industrial plants do the same thing with chemicals, acids, and dyes. Pleasure boat owners do their bit with garbage and other waste materials. Even the vast deep oceans are becoming polluted, thanks to the oil spilled from tankers and offshore drilling rigs. Not only can all these pollutants close your favorite swimming place, but they endanger marine life as well.

Restoring the purity and cleanliness of our lakes, rivers, and oceans will not be an easy task. Strict laws concerning the disposal of waste materials will have to be passed—and enforced. Equally vital will be stringent laws about where oil can be sought, and how it must be stored and transported. And, finally, all of us will have to learn to treat our lakes, rivers, and streams as natural resources, not as wet garbage dumps.

Air Pollution   As consumers, we are even more closely connected with the second type of pollution—that of the air. Most of us have, or want to have, a car. We also travel by bus and plane. Yet motor vehicles are probably the worst polluters of the air. From the exhaust of automobiles, trucks, buses, and airplanes come tons of carbon monoxide, lead, hydrocarbons, and other irritating gases and dusts.[1]

Of course, not all the air pollution is due to motor vehicles. A great deal of it is caused by sources of heat and power. It comes from the incinerators that burn our trash, for example, and from the furnaces that heat our houses and apartments. It comes from the chimneys of industrial plants and from the smokestacks of companies that produce electricity, steam, and other forms of energy. Wherever it comes from, however, the end result is the same. In many of our communities, in all our large cities, the air is fast becoming a health hazard.

William Rice, a science writer, had this to say about the air pollution that is plaguing our large cities:

> Damn it, ignore it, hold your breath until you turn blue.
> You are living in a sea of polluted air.

---

[1] The New York City Department of Air Resources estimated that in 1969, 1,304,000 tons of carbon monoxide were poured into the environment in New York City alone.

Pollution may well be one of the most serious problems consumers must face at this time.

Arthur W. Bartunek

Today, every day, you breathe in about 16,000 quarts of air, but you are not taking the stuff straight. It is liberally laced with:

Sulfur dioxide, a heavy pungent colorless irritant gas which, when combined with water and oxygen in the air, turns into a marble-dissolving, steel-eating, lung-eroding sulfuric acid mist.

Carbon monoxide, the result of man's choice of horsepower over leg power, and a gas that in high concentrations can cause death by depriving the body of oxygen.

Ozone, an unpalatable form of oxygen which can be a triple threat by causing chest pain, cough, and shortness of breath.

Nitrogen oxides, which, in large doses, damage the human respiratory system.

That stuff which the scientists like to call particulates—actually dust, dirt, soot, mini-flakes of metal, or any other bit of solid or liquid matter that can ride the air, including sometimes lead, asbestos and other poisons which, in high concentrations, can cause brain damage, cancer, and death.

These and other airborne threats fall under the general heading of air pollution. And . . . scientists know that pollution kills, although they aren't sure how and at what levels health begins to be threatened. In New York City, they [do] know that the Thanksgiving smog of 1966 killed 168, a toll that might have been far greater if it were not a holiday weekend with plants shut down and traffic at an ebb.[2]

Putting an end to air pollution will take many years and billions of dollars. Undoubtedly, we shall have to find other ways to dispose of our waste materials besides burning them. We may also have to find new sources of heat and energy—atomic power as a replacement for coal and oil, for example. However, we will have to make sure that, with these new ways and new sources, we are not just changing from one kind of pollutant to another.

Noise Pollution   We do not usually think of noise as a pollutant, but it can affect our health and well-being just as much as dirty air or dirty water. For example, people who work in exceptionally noisy places without any sort of protection for their ears may lose part or all of their hearing. So may people who spend a great deal of time taking in the amplified sounds of their favorite musicians.

The relative loudness of sound is measured in *decibels.* A person exposed to a noise level of 140 decibels will experience acute pain. It has been found that "annoyance, anxiety, constrained and explosive rage, disturbed sleep, irritability and energy draining tensions" may result from noise at lower decibel levels.[3] When you consider that a moving subway train produces 100 decibels of sound and a jet plane at close range produces 150 decibels, you can see why some people arrive at their destination with their nerves more than a little frayed.

In some ways, noise pollution may be the easiest to control. Already there are devices that can muffle the noise of engines, compression drills, and the like. Admittedly, they are often costly to install, but they do the job. What we need, then, are laws that will force people to use them.

Of course, a great deal of noise pollution is caused by individuals—screaming, shouting, leaning on the horns of their automobiles, playing

---

[2] New York *Daily News*, March 9, 1970.
[3] *New York Times*, March 12, 1970.

radios and stereos at full blast. Thus, it becomes a question of what all of us can do to make the world a quieter and more peaceful place in which to live.

Solid Waste Pollution   A fourth kind of pollution is the accumulation of junk on the landscape. Abandoned cars, for example, litter city streets or are piled in rusty heaps in the countryside. Millions of old cans lie along roadsides and spill over into parks and camp grounds. Thousands upon thousands of nonreturnable glass bottles prove to be inviting targets; invariably, they are smashed to bits. Discarded rubbish of all kinds including no-longer-wanted appliances fill city and town dumps. So great has the problem become that officials in some areas say that they are already running out of land on which junk can be stored.

Some way has to be found to keep us from being buried in trash, and various proposals have been made. In New York City, for example, it has been suggested that a "disposal fee" of 2 cents per hundred pounds be added to the cost of products packaged in paper and plastic containers. The city would collect these fees and use the money to pay for getting rid of the trash. This fee would be added to the selling price of the product, so the consumer would be paying for it. A similar idea has been proposed to rid the streets of abandoned cars. Buyers of new cars would pay an extra fee of $25, which would be used to defray the cost of destroying the car when it can no longer be used.

In recent years, the no deposit/no return bottle has become a serious problem. Since the seller no longer has any use for it, the buyer must either find some use for it or throw it away. In most cases, of course, he simply throws it out. So it is being suggested that, once again, a cash-return value be placed on containers; thus, it would become worth the trouble to return them—and they could be reused. This suggestion would lead to a reduced accumulation of trash by lengthening the period for which an object is useful. Another suggestion moves in a different direction: By producing packaging materials that will decompose quickly and completely, we could shorten the period during which an unwanted object must be stored.

It may be that our American ingenuity will find ways not only to get rid of solid waste, but also to turn trash into something of value. After all, many of our cities were built on tons of waste material. Why, then, couldn't the 100 million worn rubber tires and the 26 million glass bottles we discard every year be used in road-building? One experiment, already under way, is using ground glass in this manner. Another experiment is utilizing a mixture of grated rubber tires and asphalt for building roads. The use of such materials will not only successfully eliminate waste, but also supply us with an unlimited source of building materials. Combined with asphalt, the old tires and bottles disposed of in 1970 alone could pave a freeway so long that it would span the United States 23 times.[4]

Park Lands and Recreation

Eliminating the various forms of pollution is not the only thing we must do in order to improve the environment in which we live. Another important consideration is increasing the number of park and recreational areas in our country. Some of the best natural sites are already owned by the federal government; these could be turned into park and recreation areas. Other sites could be purchased or even leased from private owners for this purpose, and many thousands of people could use and enjoy them.

About 1850, one historian, Alexis de Tocqueville, referred to America as "that continent which still presents, as it did in primeval times, rivers that rise from never-failing sources, green and moist solitude, and limitless fields which the plowshare has never turned." It is true that there are few areas left where the fields have never been plowed, or the rivers dirtied; and fewer still where there is "green and moist solitude." However, thanks to the conservationists of earlier generations, there are, at present, a million and a half acres of beauty in the National Park System. Now, we need to set aside additional acres for our children and their children to enjoy.

Government and Personal Concern

Both the government and individual consumers are becoming more and more concerned about cleaning up the environment and preserving our natural resources. As a result, the federal government has established two agencies: The Consumer Protection and Environmental Health Service and the Council on Environmental Quality. According to its administrator, Charles C. Johnson, the former's purpose is to remind us that "the human environment consists not only of land, air, and water that give us life, but also includes the food we eat, the drugs we ingest, and all the thousands of products which we consume or use in this complicated world."[5] The latter is envisioned as the overall planning agency working with industry, with consumers, and with other government agencies to make our country a fit place to live.

Whether or not efforts of these agencies succeed will depend, to a large extent, on you. As a consumer, you will have many important decisions to make about matters that concern the environment. Will you, for example, be willing to pay more for goods that are produced in

---

[4] *Time,* March 16. 1970.
[5] *Time,* March 16, 1970.

Some natural sites are already owned by the government and will be preserved for our enjoyment.

USDA photo

factories that have installed costly antipollution equipment? Will you be willing to pay more for a car that will not pollute the air? If necessary, will you agree to prohibiting the use of all cars in cities? Will you take steps to cut down noise, even though this means that you cannot play your transistor radio on the street or turn up your stereo as loud as you might like? Are you willing to give up the kind of products and packaging that cannot easily be disposed of and therefore cause pollution problems? Will you be willing to pay higher taxes so that the government can buy and maintain more park and recreation areas?

Admittedly, these are not easy questions to answer, but how you and your fellow consumers respond to them will determine the kind of world in which you and your children will live.

SOCIETY

Many as yet unsolved social problems strongly affect the quality of our lives to as great an extent as the pollution of our environment and the waste of our natural resources do. Among the most serious of these social problems are poverty and crime. There are many reasons for being concerned about these and related problems, and our lives are touched by them in many ways: As consumers, we are concerned primarily with how they affect our buying power.

Poverty

Because a major portion of its population has a high standard of living and a great abundance of goods and services available to it, the United States has been referred to as the *affluent society*. There are many people, however, who do not have a share in this affluence. Instead, they live in poverty, subsisting on minimal incomes and doing without many of the things they really need.

According to government statistics, there are over 24 million Americans who live in poverty. Some of them are people who cannot get jobs because they lack education and training. Others have jobs, but are paid very little. There are also many elderly people who barely get by on social security and welfare payments. The money they had saved for their old age has long since vanished, thanks to the high cost of living.

It is difficult to escape from poverty. Many poor people live in slum areas where there is little chance of finding decent housing or decent jobs. Often children do not have enough to eat, and their inadequate diets cause them to be listless and inattentive in school. Teen-agers may simply drop out of school since they see little hope of being able to attain a better way of life than that of their parents. All too soon, many of them are defeated by the squalor, deprivation, and ugliness of the surroundings in which they must live.

Poverty does not only affect the poor, however. It casts its shadow on all members of our society. Many poor people live on welfare payments or on the charity supplied by private agencies. The money for these comes from the taxes and the charitable contributions that are paid for by people who have more money—but may not, themselves, be that much better off. More important, though, is the moral issue. In an affluent society, it is not right that some people should be poor simply because they are born into, then trapped by, poverty. It is one thing to be lazy and shiftless, to have no desire to learn or work. It is quite another to yearn for a decent way of life and be denied it because of the circumstances in which you live.

In 1964, Congress passed the Equal Opportunity Act. Its purpose is to raise basic education levels for the poor and to train them so that they will be qualified for a variety of jobs. This is one small step forward in the battle against poverty. Many more will have to be taken, if we are ever to have a society in which every individual has the opportunity to earn all the things that make up the good life.

Crime

Another tremendous drain on our pocketbooks is the price we pay for crime. Organized crime alone costs Americans millions of dollars every year. Millions more are added to our bills by the crimes committed by individuals—the housewife who steals a lipstick or a pair of stockings from a department store, for example, or the cashier who regularly takes "just a little" from the week's receipts. Because of their thievery, you will eventually pay higher prices for the things you buy.

Organized Crime Chances are, you will never come in contact with a member of a criminal organization; or if you do, you will not know it. Yet you are affected by the evils of organized crime in many ways—in what you pay for the meals you eat, the goods you buy, and the services you employ people to perform. Its effects reach into every home in America, through a wide variety of criminal activities, including the following:

- *Loan-sharking.* The lending of money at an excessive rate of interest is known as *loan-sharking.* Let us say, for example, that a worker needs a little extra money until payday; he borrows $10 and must pay back $12 at the end of the week. That means that he is paying 20 percent interest on the money he borrowed—if he did this over the course of a year, he would pay 1,040 percent interest!

  Far too many businessmen, in need of cash, have borrowed money from their "friendly neighborhood loan shark" at just such exorbitant rates of interest. Then when they are unable to meet the payments, criminal elements take over the business. In fact, loan-sharking is one of the main routes by which the underworld moves in on legitimate businesses. So who knows? The dairy from which you get your milk, the construction company that builds your home, the restaurant where you like to eat—any or all of them may be controlled by criminals.

- *Infiltration of unions.* Someone has said "there are just too many ways to skin the cat in the union movement for organized crime to ignore it." And, needless to say, the underworld does not ignore it. It frequently plays both sides of the street—using money and muscle to support union demands and strikes, then acting as highly paid "labor consultants" for the company in its attempt to get the unions to back down. In the end it is the criminal who gets rich, at the expense of the company, the union, and eventually the consumer.

- *Hijacking.* During the early 1970s airline hijacking became almost commonplace. Hijackers may be individuals who act on their own to secure large ransoms from the airline. More often, they are members of extremist organizations that engage in this criminal activity in order to secure the release of "political prisoners," collect large sums of money for their organizations, or impose other demands on the government.

  Hijacking adds to the cost of air travel because of the ransoms airlines must pay and the added expenses of flying planes to the destination demanded by the hijacker and taking care of hijacked passengers, personnel, and cargo. The security precautions that have been imposed to counteract the hijacking "epidemic" have caused the consumer a great deal of inconvenience and, at the same time, have increased the price of flying.

- *Protection racket.* Gangsters involved in the *protection racket* charge businessmen a weekly or monthly fee to "protect" their stores from fires, bombs, and unruly customers; and primarily to protect them from the injury to person or property the same gangsters would inflict if they were not paid. This cost, of course, is passed on to customers who buy from these merchants. Although the protection racket is particularly prevalent in poor areas, it is practiced in more wealthy sections as well, with restaurants and bars among the chief targets.

- *The numbers game.* Many people, particularly those who cannot really afford it, play the *numbers game.* This is a daily lottery in which bets of as little as 10 to 25 cents are placed on a series of three numbers. The winning numbers are determined by horse race results, and with a great many people playing, an individual has little chance of winning anything, much less winning a substantial sum.

- *Drugs.* As might be expected, organized crime is the chief source of drugs. Not only does it grow rich from the proceeds, but it is also responsible for turning many once honest people into criminals. Since it costs the average drug addict $50 to $75 a day to support his habit, he must often resort to stealing, mugging, burglarizing, shoplifting, and other crimes so that he can buy the drugs he needs.

Shoplifting and Employee Theft   Millions of dollars worth of goods are stolen from department stores and supermarkets every year. Business firms report losses of everything from typewriters and wrenches to company funds. How does this happen? Goods, money, and equipment are stolen by customers (*shoplifters*) and employees, in spite of the fact that most of them could afford to pay for what they

Millions of dollars worth of merchandise is stolen from department stores every year—and it is the consumer who ends up paying for it.

take. The reasons why these people steal are not always clear. Some of them say they do it for kicks; others regard it as a way to strike back at high prices. And there are always those who see nothing wrong in taking a little bit here, a little bit there. After all, who will miss it?

Whatever the reasons behind it, however, shoplifting and employee theft have become serious problems. In one magazine article, the situation was described as follows:

- This wave of stealing cost U.S. stores about $3 billion last year according to retailers' estimates.
- People from all walks of life are involved.
- More than half of those arrested in some parts of the country are juveniles.
- Store employees may be the greatest offenders of all.
- Cases of shoplifting have tripled since 1959.
- The average theft now amounts to about $28.
- A secret investigation of shoplifting in a major New York department store in which 175 customers were shadowed showed that 1 of every 9 stole something.
- A survey of 1,000 high school students in Delaware revealed that almost 50 percent had stolen at least once.
- To head off shoplifting, many stores are now installing TV cameras, mirrors, and other devices to keep an eye on shoppers. Store after store reports hiring more security guards.[6]

As a consumer, what should your attitude toward this problem be? Perhaps you have seen shoplifters at work, but hesitated to report them because you did not want to get them—or yourself—in trouble. Or perhaps you just felt lucky to buy something at half price, even though you felt sure the item had been stolen. Remember, though, that in the end it is you who will pay for what has been stolen. It is estimated that at least 3 percent is added to the bills of honest consumers to compensate for shoplifting and employee thefts. When security devices are bought and security police employed, that cost is also reflected in the prices you pay.

The problems of shoplifting and theft touch upon your personal values as well. Is it right to steal from a merchant who has worked hard to buy the goods with which to stock his store? Is it right to steal from a company that is responsible for its employees and to its stockholders?

---

[6] *U. S. News & World Report,* March 2, 1970.

If so, then what about stealing from family members and friends, or from a stranger on the street? Where do you draw the line?

CONSUMER RIGHTS

Suppose someone asked you whether you, as a consumer, had specific rights? If you are like most people, you would probably say, "Of course I do," most emphatically; then you would have a hard time explaining just what those rights are.

This is understandable, because while consumers always felt that they had some rights, they frequently could not get anyone to agree with them. Merchants who sold shoddy merchandise would not recognize the consumer's rights; nor would manufacturers who produced defective products. So there was the hapless consumer, out on a limb proclaiming his rights, with no one to listen to him.

In March 1962, however, the late President John F. Kennedy presented a special message to Congress. It dealt with the protection of consumer interests and emphasized the rights to which the consumer is entitled. These rights are:

- *The right to safety.* The right to be protected against the marketing of goods which are hazardous to health or life.

- *The right to be informed.* The right to be protected against fraudulent, deceitful, or grossly misleading information, advertising, labeling, or other practices, and to be given the facts he needs to make an informed choice.

- *The right to choose.* The right to be assured, wherever possible, access to a variety of products and services at competitive prices; and, in those industries in which competition is not workable and government regulation is substituted, the right to be assured satisfactory quality and service at fair prices.

- *The right to be heard.* The right to be assured that consumer interests will receive full and sympathetic consideration in the formulation of government policy and fair and expeditious treatment in its administrative tribunals.

Now you know your rights as a consumer. Remember, however, that rights are meaningless unless they are put to use. And putting them to use in solving consumer problems is your responsibility.

The Right to Safety

Of all the areas in which safety is involved, none touches our lives more than automobile safety. Death and destruction on our highways increase year by year. In part, this is due to careless drivers and heedless pedestrians. But far too many accidents are due to faults in the cars themselves—defective parts, poor design, and inadequate safety devices.

How can we cut down on the number of automobile accidents? For example, should all the states require periodic automobile inspections? Should the federal government set safety standards for automobile parts—tires, brakes, doors, and so on? Should Congress prescribe specific safety features for cars? Should you refuse to buy a car that does not have these features? What about the drivers themselves? Should those who cause accidents be required to get additional training so they will become better drivers? "Yes" answers to all these questions would mean taking away some freedom from the automobile industry and the consumer in the interest of safety. Are we ready to pay that price?

Of course, automobile safety is not our only concern. Our major airports become more dangerous each day, as passenger and freight traffic increase. How far should Congress go in providing further regulation of the air industry? How much are we, as consumers, ready to pay for needed safety measures to avoid airplane accidents?

In the area of foods, we are protected to some degree by the Food and Drug Administration, and the various agencies responsible for inspection. Yet some authorities question whether the governmental agencies have the staff or the ability to keep up with the rapid changes in food processing methods and materials. Consumers' Research had this to say on the subject:

> Concentration of manufacturers and dealers on attractiveness and neatness of packaging, and convenience, has resulted in major losses of food quality. Clever advertising, focused on nonessentials, has disarmed the American homemaker so that she accepts without question every sort of chemical modification and adulteration, without realizing what is going on. She assumes that if chemical additions to food were even potentially harmful, some government agency would promptly see to it that the adulteration was prohibited. In this she is entirely mistaken. A half-dozen Federal Government agencies (and some 50 more in the states) are concerned with food and beverage ingredients, sanitation, quality control, labeling, and advertising; their thinking and administrative practices are almost completely uncoordinated, and what the Federal agencies do is often tangled in endless delays and legalisms.[7]

What should consumers do about problems of this kind? What actions can they take or can they urge their lawmakers to take? These

---

[7] *Consumer Bulletin Annual,* Consumers' Research, Inc., 1967.

are questions that must be studied thoroughly and answered by all of us if we are to prevent needless injury and death.

The Right to Be Informed

Your second right as a consumer is the right to be protected against deceit and to be given the facts you need to make informed choices when you are buying goods and services. As you have already seen, merchants, manufacturers, and government agencies are providing consumers with more and more information about the goods and services offered in the marketplace. Also, there are increasingly stringent laws concerning false and misleading advertising and deceitful sales practices.

Why, then, don't you always get full value for the money you spend? For one thing, you may not be getting all the information you need. The label on a box of crackers, for example, may list all the ingredients that went into the crackers and offer suggestions on how they can be served, but it tells you nothing about the nutritive value (if any) of the crackers, or how long this particular box has been sitting on the grocer's shelf. Until recently the label on a dress could indicate that the fabric is "washable," but neglect to add "in cool water, with mild soap suds." So you blithely used hot water and your regular laundry detergent—and the result was a disaster!

While it is true that we need better labeling of products and more honestly informative advertisements, we also need consumers who will take advantage of the information provided, consumers who will look BEFORE they buy, consumers who will turn to government and private agencies for help when they need it.

The old saying, "A fool and his money are soon parted," still rings true. But it would not last long if all consumers made full use of their right to be informed.

The Right to Choose

President Kennedy stressed the fact that consumers should have access to a variety of high-quality goods and services that are sold at fair prices. And certainly, we have a wide variety of products to choose from—so many, in fact, that it is difficult to keep up with them. It seems as though just as soon as we learn something about one product, another takes its place. New and established products flood the market, and it is not easy to know which ones represent the best buys. Take the common can opener, for example:

There are hand-, wall-, and table-models, manually operated or electrically powered. The latter are plugged into a

The consumer has the right to a variety of merchandise from which to choose.

wall outlet or run on batteries. Some are combined with knife sharpeners. They are finished with various materials. They come in a range of colors. Some differences are functional and practical; others are merely for the sake of style. Without painstaking and time-consuming research, the consumer is hard pressed to know which differences serve function, which ones are fashion features, and which brands offer greater durability.[8]

It is not only the flood of new merchandise and the pretty packaging that makes choices difficult. Another complication is the fact that, very often, salespeople are not as well-informed as they should be. Many of them know little about the products they sell; their only interest is to make a sale so that they will get the commission—or, that failing, to get rid of the customer. A further complication is the growth of self-service stores and mail-order outlets. The consumer is forced to rely more and more on his own limited information and on labels and descriptive material that he does not fully understand.

If we are going to use fully our right to choose, we will need two things: (1) We will need more easily available and understandable facts about goods and services—on labels, packages, in advertisements, on credit contracts, in newspapers and magazines, on radio and television,

---

[8] "Consumer Issues—'66," A Report to the President from the Consumer Advisory Council.

and from manufacturers. Why, for example should the manufacturers of tires describe their products as "first line," "custom," "supertread," "belted," "radial," "wide oval," and so on? These words tell us nothing about the tires. What we should have is a factual guide that would tell us what kind of tire to buy for the kind of driving we do, and what kind of service we can expect for the dollars we spend. (2) We will need educated consumers who really use the information that is provided. There is no point in having the right to choose unless you know how to make the right choices.

The Right to Be Heard

The history of this country is filled with people who wanted to be heard. From the early colonists who protested the unfair taxes imposed on them by Great Britain to the abolitionists who condemned the practice of slavery to today's young people who are demonstrating against social injustices, we have been a country blessed with people who speak out about the issues that concern them.

Today, the voices raised in protest include both the young and the not-so-young. They are questioning the practices of some industries, the do-little or do-nothing attitudes of some government officials and agencies. Perhaps the best-known figure in the consumer protest movement is *Ralph Nader,* who first came to the attention of the nation when he almost single-handedly took on the powerful automobile industry. Why, he asked, should so many cars come off the assembly line with defects that could easily cause accidents? Why should cars have expensive chrome-plated bumpers that do not protect either the car or the people inside it? Why should farm tractors be designed in such a way that they can easily be tipped over?

Recently, Nader and his *raiders,* a group of concerned people who work with him, have begun to raise some embarrassing questions about the Food and Drug Administration. They charge, for example, that FDA staff members have covered up for the drug industry and held back information about possible dangers connected with certain drugs.

Nader's raiders are not alone—more and more people are demanding that people in business and industry think of the harm they may do to consumers and not only of the profits they want to make. Concerned consumers are attending stockholders' meetings of many businesses to ask questions that management sometimes finds difficult to answer. Just as Upton Sinclair exposed the terrible conditions of the meat packing industry at the beginning of this century, so today's concerned consumers are forcing government and business to think about what is happening—and what could happen—to people and their environment.

This growing concern for other people and the world in which we live is a strong indication that America is finally growing up.

CONSUMER RESPONSIBILITIES

You now know your rights as a consumer; but each right is also combined with certain responsibilities. Undoubtedly, you have some idea of just what those responsibilities are, but to aid you further, we will briefly recap them here. As a consumer, you have the responsibility to use the information that is available, to be quality- and safety-conscious, to use reasonable care in selecting merchandise, and to speak up.

Use the Information That is Available

It is surprising how many people do not do this. Then, when something goes wrong, they are quick to blame anyone but themselves.

Where can you get this kind of information? From many sources, such as product labels and tags; newspaper and magazine articles and advertisements; trade groups and dealer associations; federal, state, and local government agencies; voluntary consumer-interest groups; and organizations like better business bureaus and chambers of commerce.

The information is there, at least in part. It is up to you to seek it out and put it to use.

Be Quality- and Safety-Conscious

The fact is that poor quality goods will continue to be made as long as people continue to buy them. And the same is true for products that are unsafe.

Examine merchandise before you buy it. Then choose not to buy products that do not meet acceptable standards. In not buying, you are indicating your disapproval of the shoddy products.

Use Reasonable Care in Selecting Merchandise

If you want good quality merchandise at fair prices, it is important to shop with care and consideration. A good rule of thumb is to treat the merchandise as if you were the seller rather than the purchaser. If all customers followed this practice, waste due to shopworn and unsalable merchandise would be reduced and the savings would be passed on to the consumer.

Why do so many consumers avoid the responsibility of speaking up? Some of them do not want to take the time to complain about something that is wrong; others are too shy to "make waves."

If consumers do not speak up, however, how can poor quality, poor performance, and poor service ever be improved? Reputable manufacturers and merchants will usually make adjustments on products and services that have proved unsatisfactory. They want you to be satisfied with what you have bought, so that you will buy from them again.

Speak up. It is your right—and your responsibility.

CHECKING YOUR READING

1 What factors determine the prices consumers pay for goods and services?

2 Why is it true that inflation acts like a thief?

3 Why is it that Americans only recently became concerned about environmental problems?

4 What has caused our nation's waters to become so polluted?

5 What are the major sources of the gases that are polluting our country's air?

6 How can noise pollution affect the health of an individual?

7 What are some proposals for preventing our country from being buried in trash?

8 What is the purpose of the Consumer Protection and Environmental Health Service? Of the Council on Environmental Quality?

9 How does the fact that some individuals in our society are poor affect the lives of everyone in it?

10 In what ways does crime affect the pocketbook of every consumer?

11 Should a customer in a store report a shoplifter he sees at work? Why or why not?

12 List the four basic rights of the consumer that President Kennedy outlined in his message to Congress.

13 What are some of the ways a consumer's safety may be threatened by the goods he buys and uses?

14 What kinds of information about the goods he buys should be made available to a consumer?

15 List the major responsibilities that a consumer should assume.

16 Why is it that so many consumers fail to speak up when they find goods or services to be unsatisfactory?

CONSUMER PROBLEMS AND PROJECTS

1 Secure a reprint of a catalog of a mail-order house, such as Sears, Roebuck and Company or Montgomery Ward, that was issued prior to 1900. (Reprints of old mail-order catalogs are sold by many book and novelty stores and may be available from your public library.) Select at least five items that were on sale then and that are being sold today. Compare the prices quoted in the old catalog for the items you selected with the current prices shown in a copy of the most recent catalog issued by the same company. Subtract the price quoted for each item in the old catalog from the current price; then prepare a table using the headings shown below. Report on the contents of the table to your class, telling why you think the prices given in the table have increased as much as they have.

Current Price	Price Before 1900	Difference

2 Clip recent newspaper articles about pollution out of your local newspaper and prepare a bulletin board or scrapbook with the following sections: air pollution, noise pollution, solid waste pollution, water pollution. Place each article you have clipped in the most appropriate section.

3 Hobart Johnson, an engineer, receives a salary of $1,500 a month. Each year Mr. Johnson and his wife contribute his earnings for one day to the local community chest; they also give $50 a year to their church for welfare projects. The Johnsons have told their friends that they believe they have met their responsibilities for helping the poor. Do you agree with the Johnsons? Why or why not?

4 Gloria Wright's allowance never seems to be adequate. She has found a boy in her class who will lend her $1 if she will give him $1.10 within a week. (a) What is the annual interest rate Gloria is paying on this loan? (b) What kind of business is this boy actually conducting and how does it work? (c) Is this type of loan legal? Why or why not?

5 Greg Andrews' parents give him an allowance that is adequate for all his needs. He has everything he wants, and he has the money he needs to go to those places where his friends gather. Recently, Greg started shoplifting in the discount stores of his community. He says he gets a

thrill from being able to outwit the store detectives. Also, he likes to show the "crowd" the articles he has picked up. (a) Do you approve of what Greg is doing? Why or why not? (b) How do you think Greg's activities are affecting honest consumers?

6 Assume you want to purchase a portable AM transistor radio. Prepare a list of questions you want answered about the radio before you buy it. Visit three stores and ask the salesclerks the questions on your list. Write a report about this experience that includes answers to these questions: How much knowledge about radios did each salesclerk possess? What information, if any, did each salesclerk give you that you had not previously thought about? Did any of the salesclerks try to get rid of you? If so, what techniques did they use?

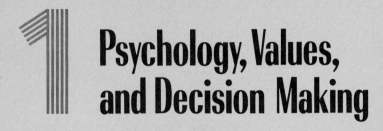

Psychology, Values, and Decision Making

LANGUAGE OF THE CONSUMER

Match each of the following numbered definitions with the correct term in the list below. Write the letter of your choice in the space provided.

a association
b come on
c compulsive spending
d conformity
e discount
f impulse buying
g individuality
h loss leader
i self-development
j self-image
k suggestion
l values

1 A product a merchant will offer for sale at its wholesale price or at a price below the amount he actually paid for it.

1 _____

2 Attitudes and opinions that consumers have about those things that are the most important to them.

2 _____

3 An advertising appeal that recognizes one's inclination to do what one's friends do.

3 _____

4 An advertising appeal that tries to link a product with people and ideas that will evoke a favorable response from the consumer.

4 _____

5 The consumer's desire to increase his knowledge, his talents, and his abilities.

5 _____

6 A gimmick or device a merchant uses to convince a consumer he is getting something for nothing or, at least, at a substantial saving.

6 _____

7 An advertising appeal that recognizes a person's desire to demonstrate unique qualities and abilities.

7 _____

8 The impulse that leads the consumer to want to buy something even though he does not know what it is he wants.   8 _____

9 The act of a consumer who purchases goods he had not planned to buy before he entered the store.   9 _____

10 An advertising appeal that uses a picture or illustration of a situation which the consumer can identify.   10 _____

BE A BETTER CONSUMER

Indicate whether each of the following statements is true or false by circling T or F in the answer column.

1 Consumer education can give you knowledge that will help you stretch your dollars so that you will be able to buy more of the things you want.   1 T F

2 Every time a consumer buys something, he is actually voting for the continued production of that product or service.   2 T F

3 A consumer's earliest values come from the opinions of his brothers and sisters.   3 T F

4 When a consumer buys food, he is satisfying his desire for physical well-being.   4 T F

5 When a consumer purchases a color television set, he is satisfying his desire for comfort and safety.   5 T F

6 As individuals grow from childhood to adulthood, they are more inclined to accept things as they are.   6 T F

7 When a man buys the same make and model car as his next door neighbor has, he is said to be "keeping up with the Joneses."   7 T F

8 When a shopper in a supermarket substitutes another brand of canned tomatoes for the brand on his list, he is said to be an impulse buyer.   8 T F

9 If a boy goes to school with 50 cents in his pocket and feels he must spend it before he returns home, he probably has a tendency toward compulsive spending.   9 T F

10 Merchants who use consumer behavior research generally try to sell goods to consumers by emphasizing their value as products.   10 T F

11 Very few teen-agers in the United States have charge accounts.   11 T F

12 When a merchant's ads urge a teen-age girl to buy fashionable clothing, he is appealing to her desire to conform.   12 T F

13 A charity ad that shows a starving child is appealing to a consumer's sense of individuality.

13 T F

14 Just before taking inventory, a merchant commonly raises the prices on the goods he has in stock.

14 T F

15 Receiving a 2 percent discount for paying cash for an item represents a real saving to the consumer.

15 T F

CONSUMER DECISIONS AND ISSUES

1 When you were a child, you usually ate Corn Toasties for breakfast. They are still your favorite dry cereal. However, they are no longer stocked in the neighborhood supermarket.

a) Why do you suppose that the supermarket no longer stocks Corn Toasties?

_____

_____

b) Assume that you have asked the store manager why he no longer stocks Corn Toasties, and he tells you that the cereal is no longer being made. Why do you suppose the manufacturer has stopped producing your favorite cereal?

_____

_____

2 Your high school has scheduled its big football game away this year. A chartered bus is to take fans to the game for $15; this amount includes transportation and a game ticket. You have a part-time job and have saved several hundred dollars. However, you plan to attend technical school next year, and you know you do not yet have nearly enough funds to pay your way through a technical school. Should you spend the $15 for the bus ticket? Why or why not?

_____

_____

_____

3 Indicate, in the spaces provided, the motives that led each of the following individuals to spend his money as he did.

a) Joe Orisine paid a "scalper" $50 for a ticket to the Superbowl game.

_____

_____

b) Mary Ditieri, a young homemaker, enrolled for a correspondence course in art appreciation.

_____

c) Lisa Walkowski purchased a bottle of French perfume to wear to the Senior Prom.

_____

d) Rod London, feeling a growling sensation in his stomach, bought some soda mint tablets at the neighborhood drug store.

_____

e) Ellen McKendrick came home from vacation with a silver charm bracelet. Her neighbor, Karen O'Connor, after seeing her friend's new jewelry, rushed to a store and bought a similar bracelet.

_____

4 High school students often buy goods and services because of the advertising they see or hear. List five items that you have bought recently in the left column of the table below; in the right column, indicate the type of advertising that influenced you to buy each of the items you have listed.

Item	Type of Advertising

5 Indicate, in the spaces provided, the principal type of appeal used by the advertiser in each of the following TV commercials:

a) A well-known Olympic swimmer is shown shaving with an electric razor.

_____

b) A local station shows a series of sketches of new houses being built for sale to young business executives.

_____

c) A housewife tells how she gets more cups of delicious

coffee at less cost from her jar of freeze-dried coffee than she did from the previous brands she has used.

___

d) A one-minute film shows a young couple flying Consolidated Airlines to Puerto Rico and, after arrival, relaxing on a sandy beach.

___

e) A car commercial urges the viewer to "move up" to the more expensive car that is shown parked in front of the entrance to a fashionable hotel.

___

6 Identify, in the spaces provided, types of sales in the following situations:
a) A gallon of milk which costs the grocer $1.32 is advertised at $1.29.

___

b) A tube of hair dressing is priced at $1.09; two tubes may be purchased for $1.10.

___

c) Just before taking stock at the end of the year, a furniture store advertises chairs and sofas at 25 to 50 percent off.

___

d) Costume jewelry is lumped together and placed on a counter near a department store's entrance; a sign on the counter reads "Prices as marked."

___

e) A men's store advertises that any buyer of a sport coat priced at $65 may purchase a pair of contrasting or matching slacks for $1.

___

7 A jeweler has recently purchased several dozen cheap imported men's wristwatches. His newspaper ads state that because of its low price one of these watches is the "best bargain in the city." Consumers are urged to hurry to his store because supplies are limited; however, the ads give very little factual information about the watches.
a) What do you suppose the jeweler hopes to accomplish by his ads?

___

b) How would you react to an ad of this type?

_____

c) How could you find out the true value of one of these watches?

_____

8 Mrs. Greene read about a new automatic washer in an ad in a national women's magazine. After reading the ad, she immediately went to an appliance store in her city and bought one of the washers. The washer has proved to be unsatisfactory for handling Mrs. Greene's laundry. Because of this experience, she believes that all advertising should be abolished; she also claims that all advertising does is to increase the cost of merchandise. Do you agree with Mrs. Greene? Why or why not?

_____
_____
_____
_____
_____
_____
_____
_____
_____
_____
_____
_____
_____
_____

Effective Consumer Behavior

LANGUAGE OF THE CONSUMER

Match each of the following numbered definitions with the correct term in the list below. Write the letter of your choice in the space provided.

a better business bureau
b *caveat emptor*
c *caveat venditor*
d chamber of commerce
e comparison shopping
f consumer testing agency

g final sales
h grades
i guarantee
j labels
k seals of approval
l seasonal bargains

1 Quality standards established by the U.S. Department of Agriculture for a number of food products.   1 _____

2 A term that means let the buyer beware.   2 _____

3 Checking of quality, services, and prices in a number of different stores in order to get the best values in the merchandise one buys.   3 _____

4 A promise to the consumer that he will be compensated in some way if the product he buys does not perform in the way it should.   4 _____

5 The sale of merchandise with the condition that the merchant will not later exchange it for something else or refund the money paid.   5 _____

6 Devices placed on merchandise by certain associations to indicate that the goods have met certain standards.   6 _____

7 An organization that examines merchandise offered for sale and reports, in written form, information useful to possible buyers.   7 _____

8 A nonprofit organization, supported by business firms, that aims to eliminate misrepresentation and trickery in business dealings.

8 _____

9 Written statements attached to many types of products that tell something about what the product contains and what care it should get.

9 _____

10 Merchandise purchased on those days or weeks when it can be bought at the lowest possible prices.

10 _____

BE A BETTER CONSUMER

Indicate whether each of the following statements is true or false by circling T or F in the answer column.

1 Spending money wisely will increase the amount of money a consumer possesses.

1 T F

2 Shoppers who buy goods in an impulsive manner frequently waste money on items they do not need or cannot use.

2 T F

3 Before a wise consumer develops a long-range shopping plan, he determines his future needs.

3 T F

4 It is a good idea for a consumer to make out a list before every shopping trip he makes.

4 T F

5 Air conditioners are an especially good buy in July.

5 T F

6 Winter coats are an especially good buy in August.

6 T F

7 If a large department store provides charge accounts, free delivery, and free alterations for its customers, it must charge higher prices for the goods it sells than if it does not provide these services.

7 T F

8 Lower grades of food are never as good to eat as top grades.

8 T F

9 The terms, "guarantee" and "warranty," have different meanings for the consumer.

9 T F

10 The single word, "guaranteed," stamped on a product means nothing.

10 T F

11 Consumers Union, in its *Consumer Reports*, describes just the good qualities of the products its tests.

11 T F

12 *Good Housekeeping* awards its seals of approval to products it tests regardless of whether or not they are advertised in the magazine.

12 T F

13 The Food and Drug Administration provides consumers with complete protection against health hazards.

13 T F

14 The wise consumer does not base his decision to buy a product simply on the opinions of others. 14 T F

15 The articles in *Changing Times,* a magazine published primarily for consumers, may be influenced by financial pressure from the magazine's advertisers. 15 T F

CONSUMER DECISIONS AND ISSUES

1 Assume that you will be continuing your education after you graduate from high school.

a) In what type of school do you plan to enroll? (Circle your choice.)

university   technical school
college   adult education center
junior college   other: _____

b) Indicate in the spaces below the items for which you will need money (such as tuition, books, clothing, etc.) and also the amount you estimate that you will need to pay for each category.

Item	Estimated Amount
_____	$ _____
_____	_____
_____	_____
_____	_____
_____	_____
Total	$ _____

c) In the space below indicate the sources from which you hope to obtain the money you will need to reach the long-range financial goal you have set for yourself.

_____
_____

2 Obtain a model number and list price for each of the appliances described in the table below; you can secure this information from the most recent issue of *The Buying Guide,* published by Consumers Union. Record this information under the appropriate headings. Then phone or visit appliance stores in your community and secure the retail price quoted for each of the items. Record this information under

the appropriate heading. You should be able to obtain the names of merchants who sell the brand names listed from the Yellow Pages of your telephone directory.

Item	Model Number	The Buying Guide Price	Local Price
Frigidaire automatic dish-washer			
General Electric side-by-side refrigerator-freezer			
Hoover upright vacuum cleaner			
Sears Coldspot room air conditioner			
Whirlpool automatic washer			
Whirlpool electric clothes dryer			

Why do the prices quoted in your community vary from those given in *The Buying Guide?*

_____

_____

_____

_____

_____

3 All of the products listed below are sold by brand names. Write the brand name that you think of first for each product in the space provided.

Product	Brand
Aspirin	
Breakfast cereal	
Canned soup	
Car (new)	
Gum	
Mouthwash	
Pen	
Shampoo	
Soft drink	
Toothpaste	

Why do you suppose that you thought of these brands first?

_____

4 The information found on product labels varies in usefulness to the consumer. Some information is often very useful; other information is of some value; and still other information is of no value. The column at the left in the table below contains descriptive terms commonly found on labels. Rate the value for the consumer of each item by placing a check (√) in the appropriate column at the right.

Descriptive Term	Value		
	Great	Some	None
Colorfast			
Dry clean only			
Easy to install			
Extra-long life			
Four-ply rated tire			
Permanent press			
Recommended by processor			
65% polyester; 35% wool			
Wash and wear			
Waterproof			

5 Mrs. Beeler says that if an appliance bears the *Good Housekeeping* Seal of Approval, she will buy the product without further investigation. Do you agree with Mrs. Beeler? Why or why not?

_____

_____

6 Mrs. Goodlander selects toys for her children which bear the seal, "Commended by *Parents' Magazine*." She claims these toys are safe and possess educational value. Do you agree with Mrs. Goodlander? Why or why not?

_____

_____

7 Magazines often contain articles that will help consumers to become better buyers. Examine a copy of each of the magazines listed in the left-hand column of the table below. On the basis of your survey, rate each of the magazines by

placing a check (√) under the heading that best describes the magazine's value to the consumer.

Magazine	Value		
	Great	Some	None
Car and Driver			
Changing Times			
Consumer Reports			
Consumers' Research Magazine			
Ebony			
Good Housekeeping			
Ladies Home Journal			
McCall's			
Newsweek			
True Story			

8 Mark Gold and Al Marino have gotten into a friendly argument about the better business bureau. Mark claims that if a consumer purchases some merchandise that proves to be unsatisfactory, all the buyer must do is call the bureau; they will then tell the merchant to replace the goods or refund the buyer's money. Al says that the better business bureau does not operate in this manner. Which boy is correct? Give reasons for your answer.

_____

_____

_____

_____

_____

_____

_____

_____

_____

_____

_____

_____

Consumer Issues

LANGUAGE OF THE CONSUMER

Match each of the following numbered definitions with the correct term in the list below. Write the letter of your choice in the space provided.

a affluent society   g pollution
b decibel   h protection racket
c infiltration   i Raiders
d inflation   j Ralph Nader
e loan-sharking   k shoplifters
f numbers game   l Upton Sinclair

1 An increase of the amount of money and credit in proportion to the amount of goods available, causing prices to rise.   1 _____

2 A criminal activity which involves charging businessmen a weekly or monthly fee to ensure that their stores will not be damaged by fire, bombs, or unruly customers.   2 _____

3 A group of concerned people who have been directing embarrassing questions at governmental protection agencies, such as the Food and Drug Administration.   3 _____

4 Customers who steal merchandise from a store.   4 _____

5 The unit for measuring the relative loudness of sound.   5 _____

6 The lending of money at an excessive rate of interest.   6 _____

7 An illegal daily lottery in which bets of as little as 10 cents to 25 cents may be placed.   7 _____

8 The best-known individual who is active in the consumer-protest movement.   8 _____

9 A term used to describe the generally high standard of living and the great abundance of goods and services in the United States.

9 _____

10 The entering of impure or unclean elements into our environment, making it an unhealthy place to live.

10 _____

BE A BETTER CONSUMER

Indicate whether each of the following statements is true or false by circling T or F in the answer column.

1 The cost of an object, for example, a man's suit, is usually less if it is made by hand than if it is made by machine.

1 T F

2 In recent years, the cost of goods and services has been decreasing steadily.

2 T F

3 The standard of living of people who have fixed incomes is reduced by inflation.

3 T F

4 The United States has an endless amount of natural resources.

4 T F

5 Pollution is one of the most critical problems consumers face.

5 T F

6 Gases from motor vehicle exhaust pipes add little pollution to the air.

6 T F

7 Amplified sounds of musical instruments may damage the listener's hearing.

7 T F

8 The use of no deposit/no return bottles is adding to the pollution of our country.

8 T F

9 Our country has an adequate number of parks and recreational areas.

9 T F

10 The continuing increase in crime is one of the reasons why consumers must pay more for goods and services than they formerly did.

10 T F

11 Teen-agers raised in poverty tend to drop out of school because they see little hope of ever bettering their positions.

11 T F

12 The effects of organized crime reach into every American home.

12 T F

13 Drug users find it difficult to obtain drugs from those engaged in organized crime.

13 T F

14 When a consumer fails to get all the information he needs

about a product he has bought, he has not received full value for the money he has spent. 14 T F

15 Manufacturers will continue to produce poor quality goods even though consumers refuse to buy them. 15 T F

CONSUMER ISSUES AND DECISIONS

1 A government expert has said that we can anticipate a 3 percent rise in the cost of living each year. Assume that this year it costs a family of four $9,000 to maintain a modest standard of living. If this official is correct, how much will it cost this family to live in the same manner five years from now?

_____

2 The sewage from your community runs into a lake where you like to swim. Recently, this notice has been posted on the beach: "Swimming Prohibited. Water Polluted." City officials are asking voters to approve a bond issue to construct a treatment plant that will prevent further pollution of the lake. Your neighbor, Louis Orsini, tells you he is going to vote against the bond issue because his taxes will be raised. Do you agree with Mr. Orsini? Why or why not?

_____

_____

_____

3 Robert and Jessica Walton retired ten years ago and live on social security. At the time they retired, the Waltons felt that they could live comfortably since they owned their home and had about $10,000 in savings. Today, the Waltons are living in poverty. They have not spent money extravagantly, and they remain in good health.

a) Why do you suppose the Waltons are now impoverished?

_____

_____

_____

b) What might the government do to help retired people like the Waltons?

_____

_____

_____

4 As a consumer, you will be affected by any efforts federal, state, and local governments make in order to control pollution. Answer each of the following questions involving your personal attitude toward some proposed government actions meant to control pollution, and give your reasons for each answer.

a) Are you willing to pay more for goods that are produced in factories that have installed costly antipollution equipment?

_____

_____

b) Are you willing to pay more for a car that will not pollute the air?

_____

_____

_____

c) Do you believe that all personal cars should be banned from city streets if this would help to control pollution?

_____

_____

_____

d) Are you willing to take steps to cut down on noise, even if you will not be able to play your stereo as loudly as you would like?

_____

_____

_____

e) Are you willing to give up buying soft drinks in no deposit/no return bottles?

_____

_____

_____

f) Are you willing to pay more taxes so that the government can buy more parks and recreational areas?

_____

_____

_____

5 More Americans are killed by automobiles each year than in any other type of accident. Many consumers are demanding that travel by car be made safer; this will require government action that will affect every owner and driver. Answer each of the following questions involving your personal attitudes toward proposed measures designed to make driving safer, and state briefly your reasons for each answer.

a) Should all states require periodic automobile inspections?

_____

_____

_____

b) Should the federal government set safety standards for automobile parts, such as tires, brakes, and doors?

_____

_____

_____

c) Should air bags be required on all newly manufactured automobiles?

_____

_____

_____

d) Should all passengers be required to have their seat belts fastened when an automobile is in motion?

_____

_____

_____

e) Should every applicant for a driver's license be required to have passed an approved driver-training course?

_____

_____

_____

6 There is an old saying, "A fool and his money are soon parted."

a) What does this saying mean?

_____

_____

_____

b) Do you agree with it? Why or why not?

_____

_____

_____

_____

_____

_____

_____

7 Compare five different AM portable transistor radios sold in a store in your area. On the table below, list the brand name, price, and special features of each brand.

Brand	Price	Special Features

How would you use the information you obtained to help make a final selection?

_____

_____

8 The record changer on your new stereo is not functioning properly, and you never hear the first few notes on a record. You have complained to the salesman at the Sound Shop, where you bought the stereo, and he has told you there is nothing he can do about it. List the steps you might have to take before you are able to get your complaint settled satisfactorily.

_____

_____

_____

_____

_____

_____

_____